Scottish Forenames

Scottish Forenames

Their Origins and History

Donald Whyte F.H.G., F.S.G. (Hon.)

Birlinn

This edition published in 2005 by
Birlinn Ltd
West Newington House
10 Newington Road
Edinburgh
EH9 1QS

www.birlinn.co.uk

ISBN10: 1 84158 398 7
ISBN13: 978 1 84158 398 3

British Library Cataloguing-in-Publication Data
A catalogue record for this book is available
from the British Library

Typeset by Brinnoven, Livingston
Printed and bound by Antony Rowe Ltd, Chippenham

INTRODUCTION

Apart from Gaelic names peculiar to Scotland and Ireland, which spread late to other parts of the country, many names treated in this book have been found in other parts of Great Britain. This applies also to Old Norse names used in the Northern Isles, Caithness, Sutherland, and in the Hebrides. Derivations from Hebrew and Greek, found in the classics and in the King James version of the Holy Bible are numerous. There are, moreover, derivations from Latin, sometimes borrowed from Greek. Old German and French names account for a significant array of forenames. Old English names which were unchanged or only slightly altered following the Norman Conquest of England in 1066 also reached Scotland.

In early times every person had only one proper name, and surnames came into use gradually. These can be divided into five classes, admittedly with some overlapping. There are those derived from the personal name of the father, more properly surnames of relationship, and patronymics come into this class. Then come hundreds of names stemming from place-names. Next come a large group derived from trades and offices, usually called occupational surnames. Into a fourth class come surnames derived from nicknames, personal traits and characteristics. These may be colloquial: exhibiting an 'official' name, and a name used by friends and neighbours. Lastly we have what can be called divergent names, flowing from a variety of sources. It is evident that forenames, or elements of these, became surnames and in comparatively recent times many surnames have become forenames.

Some explanation of patronymics may be welcomed here, as these are numerous in Scotland, especially in the Highlands and Islands. Their prevalence elsewhere in ancient times is attested by the Semitic *ben* and *bar*. In the Homeric lists of heroes they are identified by the suffixes *ades* and *ides*. Modern Greek assumed the forms *pulos*, *oula*, as in Nicopulos and Stasoula. The Romans, too, had their patronymic forms, consisting of *praenomen* (e.g. Marcus), *nomen* (e.g. Tullius) and *cognomen* (e.g. Cicero), sometimes with two other designations of the father and the tribe. With the fall of the Roman Empire, the system declined and men came to be known simply by the name of the father, e.g., Hugo *filius* Walterus, meaning Hugh, son of Walter. The Slavonic forms were *vich, vitch, vic, ich* and *ov* (off) as well as the Romanian *escu*. The Teutonic nations added *sen* or *son* to the personal name, while the Saxons added *ing*, as in Atheling, meaning Athel's son. In Wales a form of the Celtic *mac* was adopted, which the Cambrians made *mab* or *map*, shortened to *ap*, thus, to give an example, Ap Richard, which became the surname Pritchard. The Irish, being mainly Celts, used *mac*, 'son of', as a prefix but often found charm in *ua*, originally grandson, but by an extension of meaning any descendant. It is found written as *Ua* by Latin and English writers, and still more often as O, which is a common prefix of Irish surnames.

Surnames begin to appear in early Irish chronicles, and in Adamnan's *Life of Saint Columba*: thus the *mac* prefix was adopted in the Highlands and Western Isles. However, until a late period, only the chiefs bore the full name. The clansmen used patronymics, and their love of genealogy and description produced forms such as Dhomnuill mac Chalum 'ic Alastair 'ic Iain Ban (Donald, son of Malcolm, son of Alexander, Son of Fair John). The clan chiefs adopted their names from a remote ancestor remembered for some brave deed or historic event, whose name became the fixed surname. The MacDonalds, the largest clan, derived their name from Donald, Lord of Islay and Kintyre, who was son of Reginald, son of the mighty Somerled, *Regulas of the Isles*.

Dr Samuel Johnson learned of the system when he toured the Highlands and Islands with James Boswell in 1773. He afterwards wrote:

Where the races are thus numerous, and thus combined, none but the chief of a clan is addressed by his surname. The Laird of Dunvegan is called MacLeod, but other gentlemen of the same family are denominated by the places where they reside, as Raasay, Talisker. The distinction of the meaner people is by their Christian name. In consequence of this practice, the late Laird of MacFarlane, an eminent genealogist, considered himself disrespectfully treated if the common addition was applied to him. 'Mr MacFarlane,' he said, 'may with propriety be many, but I and only I, am MacFarlane.'

The person who had addressed the chief as 'Mr MacFarlane' was General Wade. Johnson, however, could not bring himself to use the surname only, as he thought it was the way in which, in all other places, inferiors were addressed. Some Gaels had by that time adopted the surname of their chiefs, but patronymics persisted in remote areas such as the Outer Hebrides, as late as the early part of the nineteenth century.

The use of surnames became more frequent during the reign of Malcolm 'Canmore' (1057–93), but many landowners assumed no surname until considerably later. Anglo-Normans and Flemings acquired lands in Scotland, and distinguished themselves by the appellation of their lands. Their example was gradually followed by natives. In small rural communities personal names were sufficient, and the process grew with an increase in population. In areas where people bore the same forename and surname, colloquial naming developed. It is easy to see how William, the postman, became 'Postie Willie', but not why there should be a 'Postie Annie', his daughter, but forms like these were understood in their own communities. In Gaeldom, distinctions such as Roderick *Mor*, Roderick *Og*, and Roderick *Dhu*, were made.

Although Gaelic Christian names survived in Lowland Scotland long after the Gaelic language ceased to be spoken, by the Reformation these were out of fashion, except for old royal names such as Kenneth, Malcolm and Duncan. The names of saints survived – Patrick, John, Mungo and Ninian. William fared better, and other royal names like Alexander, Robert and James appear in the parochial registers. Archibald, an Old German name, reached Scotland through Norman and Flemish influence, and other names which remained popular were Adam, Alan, Andrew, Arthur, David, Gavin, Gilbert, George, Hugh, Matthew and Walter. Curiously, George was uncommon in England before the Hanoverian succession, despite being the name of the national saint.

In the Northern Isles, nicknames were used at an early period. The equivalent of the Gaelic *Og* in the Orkneys was *'Barn'*, or as we might say, 'Younger' or 'Junior'. Some of the nicknames are well known owing to the part played in history by the bearers: *Silkiskjegg silkisbegg*, 'Siltrygg Silky-beard', *Harair Harffagri* 'Harald Fair Hair', and *Magnus berfoettr*, 'Magnus Barelegs'. Names derived from the father became common in the Shetlands, and fixed surnames were rare. Examples of Shetland male names are Christopherson, Bernardson and Henryson. Girls were given names such as Androisdochter, Erasmusdochter and Williamsdochter. This form of nomenclature survives in Iceland, and an example follows:

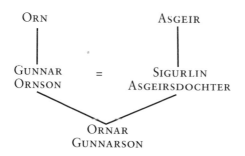

It is often said that the Scots had a traditional naming pattern which was more or less rigid, but while it was widespread it was not so unyielding as some genealogists have maintained. Here we are referring to the custom of naming the first two boys and the first two girls in a family after the four grandparents. A good example is the family of Donald Sage, author of *Memorabilia Domestica: Parish Life in the North of Scotland* (published 1889):

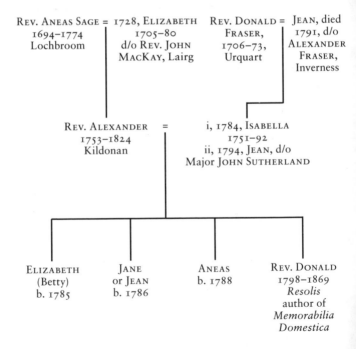

REV. ANEAS SAGE = 1728, ELIZABETH REV. DONALD = JEAN, died
1694–1774   1705–80   FRASER,   1791, d/o
Lochbroom   d/o REV. JOHN   1706–73,   ALEXANDER
                     MACKAY, Lairg   Urquart   FRASER,
                                                               Inverness

REV. ALEXANDER = i, 1784, ISABELLA
1753–1824   1751–92
Kildonan   ii, 1794, JEAN, d/o
                  Major JOHN SUTHERLAND

ELIZABETH   JANE   ANEAS   REV. DONALD
(Betty)   or JEAN   b. 1788   1798–1869
b. 1785   b. 1786   *Resolis*
                                             author of
                                             *Memorabilia
                                             Domestica*

The elder son was named after the paternal grandfather, and the younger after the maternal grandfather. The elder daughter was named after the paternal grandmother, and the younger after the maternal grandmother. This was the usual preference, but occasionally the mother had the first choice of names for her children. On the Isle of Colonsay, John, son of Angus Bell and Peggy (Margaret) McFadyen, married Margaret, daughter of Archibald McCalder and Catherine Blue. Their first four children were Catherine, born 1837, named after the maternal grandmother; Archibald, born 1838, named after the maternal grandfather; Angus, born 1840, named after the paternal grandfather, and Margaret, born 1844, named after the paternal grandmother. The fact that the first two were named after the wife's parents (the second not after the husband's parent) is unusual, and perhaps indicates that Margaret McCalder was a strong personality.

Frequently third sons and daughters were named after the parents, if they did not have the same name as *their* parents, but this was not always the case, and aunts and uncles were chosen alternately from both sides of the family. However, the system allowed other choices, and occasionally names of special friends were given, and even notable events sometimes influenced the baptismal name. The *Cromdale and Inverallon Old Parochial Registers*, in the custody of the Registrar General for Scotland, record the baptism of Ludovick, son of Collin Lawson and Mary Grant in Clashindunan, 4 November 1703, named after Ludovick Grant of Grant. The *Dyke Old Parochial Registers* record, on 20 September 1772, the baptism of Margaret, daughter of William Rose (name of spouse not entered), named after Mrs Margaret Russell of Earlsmill and her daughter of the same name. A week later, the same register records that Margaret, daughter of Donald McInnon (sic) in Cottartown of Brodie (name of wife not entered) was named after Lady Margaret Brodie.

The national bard, Robert Burns, and 'Bonnie' Jean Armour, did not follow the traditional naming pattern. Their first two children were named after themselves, Robert and Jean, twins, born 3 September 1786. The daughter died 3 March 1788. Burns had married Jean Armour by declaration, literally under the 'Green Thorn Tree', and they were called before the Kirk of Session of Mauchline, 5 August 1788, for having contracted an irregular marriage. They were rebuked and gave a solemn oath to adhere to one another as husband and wife during life. They had another set of twins who seemed to have died in infancy, unnamed. Their next child was Francis Wallace, born 18 August 1789, and named in honour of the bard's literary friend, Mrs Dunlop of Dunlop, and Francis Grose (1731–91), the English antiquary, who visited Burns when he lived at The Isle while his farmhouse at Ellisland was being built. This child died in 1803. Next came William Nicol Burns, born 9 April 1791, named after William Nicol, Latin master of the High School of Edinburgh, who accompanied the bard on his Highland tour in 1787. Elizabeth Riddel Burns, born 21 November 1792, was named in honour of Mrs Riddel of Glenriddel. This daughter died aged three. James Glencairn Burns, third surviving son of Robert and Jean, was born in 1794 and named after the deceased James [Cunningham], 14th Earl of Glencairn, for whom the poet penned a *Lament*.

Maxwell Burns, born the day of his father's funeral in July 1796, was named after Dr William Maxwell, the family physician in Dumfries. He, too, died young.

In many parishes it was customary to name the first child baptised by a new minister after him, even if the child was a girl. Rev. Hugh Meiklejohn (later Professor of Ecclesiastical History at the University of Edinburgh) was ordained minister of the West Lothian parish of Abercorn on 22 December 1791. On the same day he baptised a daughter of George Hay and Elizabeth Carlaw in Crawstane, and she was named Hughina. The practice of adding 'ina' to male names was not unusual, especially when a boy had been wanted, and it produced names such as Adamina, Alexandrina, Donaldina, Douglasina, Thomasina, Murdina and Williamina. They were usually simply known as Ina. The practice is not now popular except in the Outer Hebrides.

Historical events were also commemorated in given names. *The Kells Old Parochial Register*, 28 June 1838, records the baptism of Victoria, daughter of Robert Johnstone, joiner in New Galloway, and his wife Mary McCormack, the date being that of the coronation of Queen Victoria. Children are sometimes named after particular days, e.g. girls born on 19 April, 'Primrose Day', have been called Primrose.

Up until about 1830, it is unusual to find more than one Christian name recorded, although more than one may have been used. Mary Beatrice Anna Margaret Frances Isabella, daughter of John, 8th Lord of Elphinstone, was born at Edinburgh, and named after the Duchess of York, who was then in Scotland. She was Mary Beatrice Eleanor

D'Este, daughter of Alphonso, Duke of Modena, and Laura Martinozzie, who married James, Duke of York, afterwards King James VII and II. She is usually referred to as Mary of Modena. One early instance of giving more than one name occurs at Monkton in Ayrshire, where Glencairn Dalrymple Flatchert, son of David Flatchert, wright, was born and baptised on 1 June 1766. One wonders what prompted the choice of names. Sometimes two names have been conjoined, as in the case of Adahbyron, daughter of George Nicolson and his wife Elisabeth, in Ulnabreak, Tingwall, Shetland, named after Lord Byron in 1838. It is not unusual to find emigrant Scots, especially to the USA, adopting the mother's surname as a middle name. John Pennycook, from Cluny parish, Perthshire, emigrated to Morgan County, Illinois, in 1834, and actually changed the family name to his mother's maiden surname of McDonald, presumably because it identified the family more clearly as Scots.

Foundlings were frequently given the name of the town or village in which they were abandoned, or the name of a sponsor (often the person who had agreed to foster the child), minister or ruling elder present at the baptism. A foundling exposed at the Mealmarket of Edinburgh, 'naked as it came in the world', was named William Edenburgh, when baptised on 5 December 1690. An infant girl found in Glasgow was baptised on 23 February 1735 and named Anne Glasgow. In Perthshire, a female child found at Conyachan was sponsored by the Misses Campbell of Monzie, baptised on 1 August 1788, and named Rosina. They took the child into their care. A boy found at the door of John Todd, a farmer in Long

Livingston, on the morning of 4 August 1800, was baptised two days later and named George Livingston, after
the reigning monarch and the parish of Livingston.

While sponsors were a feature of baptism, in many
parts of the country it was thought to bring good fortune
to the child if there were 'name-fathers' or 'name-mothers', i.e. witnesses who bore the Christian name being
given to the child. At Edinburgh on 22 October 1595,
Robert, son of James Skaithmure, chirurgeon, had a
son baptised and named Robert. The witnesses were
Robert Auchmouty, chirurgeon, and Robert Walgrave,
painter. This custom survived longer in the north, and
the *Elgin Old Parochial Registers* record the baptism on
8 November 1757, of Ann, daughter of James Richards,
merchant, and his wife Lillias Spark. The 'name-mothers'
were Ann Calder and Anne Davidson. George Charles
was a witness. Alexander, son of John Nairne, tenant in
Dunvarency in Ferintosh, was baptised at Urquhart, 16
November 1787, when the 'name-fathers' were Alexander
Brodie, MP for Nairn, Alexander Hay, Sheriff Clerk of
the county and Alexander Rose of Fleminetown, who
went to Jamaica.

Pet names and short forms should be kept in mind
when consulting indexes to records, as many persons
were known by a name other than their baptismal one.
This is particularly important when checking death
records as wrong information can be given to registrars
by people still suffering from shock through the loss
of a loved one. Alexander could be Alastair at baptism,
or vice-versa, and known by the form not on the birth
certificate. Agnes might be recorded as Nancy. It has

also to be remembered that many names share the same short form. Ag can be a pet name for Agnes, likewise for Agatha; Fred and Freddy may appear for Alfred or Frederick; Bell or Bella can mean Annabel or Isabel; Gus can stand for Angus or Augustus, and Tina can mean Christina or Clementina. More examples are in the text of this book. Stacey as a surname derives from Eustace, but as a forename it stems from Anastasia, and there are variant spellings.

Many changes have taken place in the present century, especially since the close of World War II, and it is now fashionable to ignore old naming patterns and even names which have been much used in families. The new generation of minor royalty and major aristocracy, who have married outwith their traditional breeding grounds, have not been able to resist such patterns. Lady Tess, daughter of the 27th Duke of Norfolk, married Roderick Balfour, an investment director, in 1971, and the names of their four daughters are Willa, Kinvara, Candida and Marie.

Some biblical names have survived well, e.g. Rebecca, Hannah, Rachel, David, Andrew and Mark, as well as some names used in the Middle Ages (476–1492), especially after the Norman Conquest of England in 1066. However, literature has had a powerful influence on naming, and the effects of the cinema over the past century cannot be underestimated, especially from around 1912, when the silent pictures appeared with captions and music. The effects of radio during the same period stimulated demand for sound, and the first 'talkies' were shown in 1927. The working classes, perhaps not so much influenced by literature, began to give children the names of film stars. Many people copied the dress of the actors. Women changed hairstyles and made greater use of cosmetics. Television has also had a profound effect on the choice of names for children.

Even the stars themselves have not escaped the influence of films. Humphrey Bogart (1899–1957), one of the 'Hollywood greats', named a daughter Leslie as a compliment to actor Leslie Howard (1893–1943), who helped him when he was still unknown. John Wayne (1907–79), who was 'Uncle Ethan' in the classic western *The Searchers*, which he considered his finest role, named a son Ethan. Scottish actor James Cosmo (James Copeland, Jr.), now living at Twickenham, and Annie, his second wife, also named a son Ethan, from the same film. Scots actor Robbie Coltrane and his wife, Rhona, named a son Spencer, after another 'Hollywood great', Spencer Tracey (1900–67). The naming of children will no doubt continue to change, either through the invention of new forenames or by alterations in the spelling of current names.

This book covers the most popular names in Scottish families, with some others entered for historic reasons. It differs from others in print at this time. No apologies are made for quoting the names of early ecclesiastics and of members of the nobility and landed gentry before the seventeenth century, when information about more humble folk is very scarce. Similarly no excuses are made for non-inclusion of tables of the most popular names in different years, simply because they usually vary from one decade to the next, and what seems worthwhile is included in the main text. The minority who seek such information are respectfully referred to information from the General Register Office (GRO) on the Internet, presented as Web pages on the Government Information Service server. It is ongoing, and the GRO's site can be found at http://www.open gov.uk/gros/groshome.htm.

Sincere thanks are extended to the staff of the General Register Office, Edinburgh for assistance over a number of years which has contributed greatly to this work. Thanks are also extended to Mr D.R. Torrance, Chairman of the Council of the Scottish Genealogy Society, and to various colleagues, members of the Association of Scottish Genealogists and Record Agents, for comments and/or assistance.

Donald Whyte

ABBREVIATIONS

Gael.	Gaelic
Gr.	Greek
Heb.	Hebrew
Lat.	Latin
NT	New Testament
O.E.	Old English
O.Fr.	Old French
O.G.	Old German
O.Nor.	Old Norse
OT	Old Testament
c.	Circa (about)

In the main text, names in capital letters indicate an entry under the name shown.

A

Aaron (m) Heb. 'great height'. Aaron (OT, Exodus 28:1) was the brother of Moses who was commanded to invest and clothe himself and his sons in the priesthood. An early Aaron in Britain (as recorded by Bede) was martyred along with Julius, both citizens of Chester, for the Christian faith in AD 305. Sir Walter Scott, in his novel *Guy Mannering*, uses the name for Rev. Aaron MacBriar, chaplain to Donohoe Bertram's mother, and he is turned out of doors by Donohoe after a quarrel about the good graces of a milkmaid. In spite of this mention by the great novelist, Aaron was almost unknown in Scotland until modern times, but is now quite popular. This is difficult to explain, but possibly screen credits for the American Aaron Spelling are responsible. Variants are Aaran, Arran and Aaren. *Aaron's Beard* is a name given to the plant Great St John's Wort.

Abigail (f) Heb. 'father rejoiced'. In the scriptures Abigail is the wife of the ill-natured Nabal, whose rudeness to ten young men sent to him by DAVID brought upon him an armed raid by the latter. Abigail diverted him from his murderous purpose and after 'the Lord smote Nabal' and he died, she married David (OT, 1 Samuel 25:20–3). The name was popularised by Abigail Hill (Mrs Mashum), waiting woman to Queen Anne, and was employed by Swift, Fielding and others in their novels. The name, however, was used in Scotland before that period (1702–14). Abigail, daughter of Sir John Carmichael, Younger of that Ilk, and Margaret Douglas, married before 13 August 1613, John Hume, Younger of Huttonhall. The forename is still in use, and the old short forms, GAIL and GAYLE, are now independent. Moreover, Abbi, Abbie and Abby, formerly only pet names, are often given names.

ABRAHAM (m) Heb. 'father of many'. The name of the OT patriarch was changed when he was ninety years old from Abram, 'high father', to Abraham, 'father of many'. He was the son of Terah, who died between the Euphrates and the Tigris and founded a dynasty. His first child, Eliezer, was by an illegitimate slave. Sarah, his wife, was childless, and she gave him her Egyptian slave, Hagar, who bore him Ishmael. By two daughters of his nephew, Lot, he had sons Moab and Ben-ammi. Eventually Sarah bore him a son, Isaac (OT, Genesis 21:2–3), who married REBECCA. The patriarch has a place in Muslim as well as in Jewish and Christian tradition. The name was popular in Lowland Scotland after the Reformation, but is not now in the top one hundred boys' names. In America, Abraham Lincoln (1809–65), 16th President, gave the name prominence. Bram is a Dutch contraction of the name. Pet names are Abe and Abie.

ADA (f) Originally a short form of Germanic names beginning with Adal, such as ADALINE, Ada came to be used independently. It came early to Scotland. Henry of Huntingdon and Northumberland married in 1139

Ada, daughter of William Warenne, 2nd Earl of Surrey, and had six children, two of whom, MALCOLM and WILLIAM, became Kings of Scots. Their daughter Ada married in 1161 Florence III, Count of Holland. Ada de Fraser signed the *Ragman Roll* in 1296. This royal name was not favoured by the Bruces, and lost ground in the fourteenth century. It staged a revival in the mid-nineteenth century but is not widely used.

ADAH (f) Heb. 'ornament'. The scriptures give Adah and Zillah as wives of Lamech, son of Methuselah (OT, Genesis 4:19). Another Adah, daughter of Elon the Hittite, married Esau (Genesis 36:2). The name was never as popular as ADA, with which it is sometimes confused.

ADAM (m) Heb. 'red', possibly from a ruddy complexion. The name of the first man according to the world's best-seller (OT, Genesis 1:19). Adam is said to have lived for 930 years. The name was popular in the Middle Ages. Adam, Abbot of Cupar, is on record in 1190. Adam, an abbot of Melrose, became Bishop of Caithness in 1213. In Ireland, Adam gave rise to Adamnan, and the most famous of the name was Abbot of Iona and biographer of St Columba. In Gaelic, *Gilla Adhamnain* became *Gilleownan*, a favourite name among the clans of the West Highlands and Islands. The MacLeans are known as 'Clan Gille-eon'. Adam has been well used in Scotland and is still within the top forty names. Sir Adam de Swinton, who died in 1229, is mentioned in a donation made by his widow, Fluria, to the monastery of Soltray, before 1232. Dr Adam Ferguson (1723–90),

Professor of Natural History at Edinburgh, lived at Sciennes, Edinburgh, where in 1787 the young Walter Scott is said to have met Robert Burns. Adam Smith (1723–90), born at Kirkcaldy, is famous as a pioneer political economist. A number of surnames have stemmed from Adam, including Adam, Adams, Adamson, Addison and Atkins.

ADAMINA (f) Feminine form of Adam, not now common.

ADELA, ADELE (f) O.G. 'of noble rank', as with Adelaide. Adele de Grand, sister of the Lord of Alost, in Flanders, married Baldwin, son of Guy, Count of Boulogne. Their son Count EUSTACE I, was a companion of William the Conqueror, and married Maud de Louvain, granddaughter of Charles, Duke of Lorraine, the last direct heir of the Carolingian rulers of France. Adela was an early form, and the name of the Conqueror's fourth daughter. Through him the name came to England. The French form, Adele, became more popular in Scotland.

ADELAIDE (f) O.G. *Adaheit*, 'of noble rank'. Adelaide is the French form, and was common on the continent for centuries. It made its appearance in Britain in the eighteenth century and was boosted in 1830 when Adelaide of Saxe-Coburg became Queen Consort of King William IV. Adelaide in South Australia is named after her. Adelaide Harriet Melville (1831–98) was a daughter of John, Earl of Leven and Melville. In modern times the name is more widely used under pet forms such as ADELA, ALICE and the German Heidi.

ADELINE (f) Like ADELAIDE and ADELA / ADELE, the name derives from the O.G. word meaning 'of noble rank'. It was cited in England in the *Domesday Book*, but not much used in the later Middle Ages. The name became ALINE in some cases, but the latter name appears also as a diminutive of ALICE. Arleen and ARLINE are sometimes variants, but the latter has other connotations.

ADOLPH (m) O.G. *athal-wolfa*, 'noble wolf'. This appears often in its Latinised form, Adolphus. It is believed that the name came to Britain as a consequence of the Hanoverian succession of 1714, but in fact the name came to Scotland as a result of many Scots having fought in the early seventeenth century under Gustavus Adolphus of Sweden. Sir Lucius Cary, 2nd Viscount Falkland, named a son Adolphus in 1639, doubtless after the Swedish monarch. The name is now rare, as is the feminine Adolpha.

ADRIAN (m) Lat. *Hadrianus*, 'man from Adria', an area of Northern Italy. The Roman Emperor Hadrianus visited England in AD 119 and promoted the wall between Solway and Tyne. This was also the name of several popes, one of whom, Adrian IV (Nicholas Breakspear, died 1159), was an Englishman. St Adrian, died 870, is said to have come from Hungary, but more likely from Ireland, to Fife. He settled with St Monans, who was killed by Norsemen. Adrian sought refuge on the Isle of May, but suffered the same fate. The name has always been used sparingly in Scotland. Feminine forms are ADRIANNE, Adriana and Adrienne.

ADRIANNE Feminine form of ADRIAN.

AEMILIUS (m) Lat., the name of a Roman plebeian clan. Boccaccio, a fourteenth-century Italian writer, used

Emilia, popularising the name in the Middle Ages, and Chaucer borrowed it in the form Emelye. Aemilius, son of Alexander Simpson, a Dingwall schoolmaster, served in Canada with the Hudson's Bay Company, and in 1839 was sent to the Sandwich Islands. He wrote *The Life and Times of Thomas Simpson, the Arctic Explorer* (London, 1845) about his brother. The feminine forms are AMELIA and EMILY.

AENEAS (m) Gr. *Aineias*, 'praiseworthy'. It was the name of the Trojan hero whose exploits were glorified by Virgil and others. A man of this name is mentioned in the scriptures (NT, Acts 9:33–34) as having kept his bed in Lydda, being sick of the palsy, and was cured by PETER. In ancient Ireland the name was synonymous with *Aonghas* or ANGUS. Although in Scotland the name has been considered independent, it was used in the same way in Gaeldom. Rev. Aneas MacAulay (1704–60) was minister of Applecross, and his son Aneas or Angus (1759–1827), physician and preacher, went to P.E.I., Canada, in 1803, where he was agent for Lord Selkirk. It is now less used than Angus.

AGATHA (f) Gr. *Agathe*, 'good'. The name was popular in Roman times and in the Middle Ages, but is sparingly used today. Agatha, widow of Edward the Exile, came to Scotland with her son Edgar *Atheling*, and her daughters Margaret (who married Malcolm Canmore) and Christian. Agatha, daughter of Robert de Brus, a Yorkshire baron, and ancestor of Robert I, King of Scots (1306–29), married Ralph, son of Ribald, Lord of Middleham. In Scott's *Count Robert of Paris*, Agatha is the name given to the Saxon Bertha by the Lady of Aspramonte as being less 'uncouth' and 'heathenish'. The best-known bearer of the name in modern times was the crime novelist Agatha Christie (1891–1975). Ag and Aggie are pet names.

AGNES (f) Gr. word meaning 'pure' or 'chaste'. St Agnes was a third century virgin martyr. The name is found in the Latinised forms *Agnetis* and *Agneta*, but appears also as Annie, Annice, Annes. The name Agnes was long popular in Scotland, and is sometimes synonymous with NANCY. Agnes Craig (1759–1841), called Nancy, married James MacLehose, who went to Jamaica. She was the 'Clarinda' of the poet Burns, and inspired his exquisite song, 'Ae fond kiss'. Ag and Aggie, shared with AGATHA, are pet names, also Nessie and Nessa, used also as short forms of VANESSA. See also SENGA.

AIDAN (m) Gael. 'fire', is of Irish origin. Aidan, son of Gabhran, was King of Scots 574–606, and was inaugurated by St Columba. Another Aidan, of Irish extraction and a monk of Iona, became Bishop of Lindisfarne in 635 and died in 651. The name was revived by the Oxford or Tractarian movement in England in the Early Victorian period, but later lost ground. Nevertheless, the name has staged a revival in Scotland in recent years, twenty-nine having been recorded in 1990. The feminine form is EITHNE.

AILEEN (f) Gael. 'Eilidh', an Irish form of HELEN, and becoming popular in Scotland. The French form ELAINE is also in use (Irish Eibhlin, or Aibhlin), and Eilean, Eilleen, Ilean, Ileene and Ilene have been

7

recorded. Pet forms include Eily and Eiley. The Gaelic form *EILIDH* is well used.

AIMEE (f) Variant of AMY.

ALAN *see* ALLAN.

ALANA (f) A modern feminine form of ALAN, which has superseded Alanina. It is now within the top one hundred girls' names registered in Scotland, and appears also as Alanna, Allana and Allene.

ALASDAIR, ALISDAIR, ALISTAIR and ALISTER *see* ALEXANDER

ALBERT (m) O.G. *athal-berhta*, 'noble bright'. Equivalent to the O.E. *Aethelbeorht*, or Ethelbert, the name of a Kentish king who welcomed St Augustine in 597, when he landed at Thanet with other monks, and became Archbishop of Canterbury. Alban was in use in the Middle Ages, but is probably not a variant. The name was uncommon in Britain before 1840, when Queen Victoria married Albert, Prince of Saxe-Coburg and Gotha. The surnames Albert and Albright are derived from it. The Gaelic form is *Ailbert*, and short forms are Al, Bert and Bertie. Albertina has been recorded as a feminine form, but Alberta is the usual style. An 'Albert' is a kind of watch-chain, so called from Albert, consort of Queen Victoria, who was presented with one at Birmingham in 1849.

ALEXANDER (m) Gr. from a word meaning 'defender', or 'helper'. The name is of great antiquity. Alexander the Great (356–323 BC) was the conqueror of many nations and diffused the language and civilisation of Greece. An

Alexander is mentioned in the Bible (NT, Mark 15:21) as a son of Rufus and compelled to carry the cross of Christ. It was also the name of several saints and popes. Three Scottish kings were named Alexander. The first was fourth son of Malcolm Canmore and the saintly Queen Margaret, and he married SIBYL, natural daughter of Henry I of England. Alexander II (1198–1249) was son of William the Lion, and was twice married. By his second queen he had a son, Alexander III, accidentally killed near Kinghorn in 1286. Alexander was also the name of three Czars of Russia. Alexander Archibald, an American divine of Scottish descent who died in 1851, was Professor of Theology at Princeton. Edinburgh-born Alexander Graham Bell (1847–1922) emigrated to Canada in 1870 as a teacher of the dumb. He is credited with having invented the telephone (patent accepted, 1876). The name is still within the top forty boys' names registered in Scotland. The Gaelic forms, ALASDAIR, ALISDAIR, ALISTAIR and ALISTER are also well used. Short forms are Alex and Alick, and pet forms include Sandy, Eck, Eckie and Ecky. The most popular feminine form is ALEXANDRA.

ALEXANDRA (f) The usual feminine form of ALEXANDER. The name became popular after the marriage of the Prince of Wales (afterwards King Edward VII) and Princess Alexandra of Denmark in 1863. Variant forms, not much in evidence today, are Alexanderina and Alexandrina, but Alexina is in use, as also the Italian diminutive, SANDRA. Pet forms are Lex, Lexi and Lexy.

ALEXIS (f, m) from the Gr. word meaning 'helper'. This is a common name in Russia and has been occasionally used in Britain and Russia for both males and females. It is sometimes thought of as a short form of ALEXANDRA. Alexis is the patron saint of hermits and beggars.

ALFRED (m) O.E. *aelf-raed*, 'elf counsel'. Alfred the Great was a ninth-century Saxon king of England, mentioned by Bede. The name *Ealdfrith*, 'old peace', a seventh-century king of Northumbria, appears here and there as Alfred. The name was Latinised *Aluredus*, giving rise to Alured and then to Averty, which survives as a surname. Alfred evolved differently from FREDERICK, but shares the same short forms Fred and Freddy. Alf is a pet name, and Alfreda is a rare feminine form.

ALICE (f) O.Fr. *Alis* of *Adalis* appears in German as Adalheidis, meaning 'nobility'. William Fritz Duncan, a Scottish military leader at the Battle of the Standard in 1138, married Alice de Romelie, an English heiress. The name was quite prolific until the early nineteenth century and is still in current use: there were about forty Scottish registrations in 1990. In Scott's novel, *The Betrothed* (1825), Alice was an attendant, who, with Rose Flammock, accompanied EVALINE Berenger, when confined in her own apartment by Henry II. Alice of Bower appears in his *Black Dwarf*, and in *Peveril of the Peak*, Alice is 'a dowdy slipshod wench', the drudge of John Whitecraft's inn. In the *Bride of Lammermoor*, Alice is an 'ancient domestic'. ALISON, once a diminutive form, is popular.

ALICIA (f) Latinised form of ALISON. Alicia, daughter of Sir Colin Campbell of Lochawe, married in 1371 Allan Lauder of Hatton. Alicia (or Alison) Cockburn, was the authoress of the beautiful lyric, 'I've seen the smiling of fortune beguiling', one of the sets of *The Flowers of the Forest*. Alisha and Elisha have been noted in Ireland as incorrect spellings of Alicia. Variant forms are Alycia and Allissa.

ALINE (f) A diminutive of ADELINE, now used independently.

ALISDAIR *See* ALEXANDER.

ALISON (f) In the present century Alison has overtaken its parent name, ALICE, and also the Latin form, ALICIA. Variants are Allyson and Alyson, and pet names are Alley and Allie. Occasionally Elsie is used. Allison or Ellison Begbie was an early friend of the poet Burns, and is said to have inspired two or three songs. In Scott's *Kenilworth*, Allison is one of two 'aged crones' who kept the apartments of the Countess of Leicester.

ALISTER *See* ALEXANDER.

ALLAN, ALLEN (m) The name of a Welsh and Breton saint, sometimes given as Alan, but of uncertain meaning. Gaelic scholars have suggested 'rock' and 'noble'. The name came into Britain with Alan, Earl of Brittany, who was given lands in Richmondshire by the Conqueror. Alano or Alan, a monk of Durham, *c.* 1148, contemporary with Alan, son of Waldeve and brother of Cospatrick and Dolphin, witnessed charters and held lands in Cumberland. Alano *filius* Raulfi witnessed a charter of land in Oxnam, 1152/53. Alan Fitz Flaald was the father of Walter Fitz Alan, whose son Alan Fitz Walter was the first to take the name Stewart from the office of High Steward of Scotland. He was the ancestor of the Stewart kings and of several noble families. The popularity of the name down through the ages is evidenced by the number of evolved surnames, which include Allan, Allen, Allain and Alanson. Feminine forms are ALANA, Alaine, Alleyne and Alena. Allanina, daughter of Roderick Campbell, blacksmith, married at Stornoway, in 1874, John Nicholson. This feminine form is now out of fashion. The male Gaelic form is *Ailean*. In Scott's *Rob Roy*, Allan is one of the Highlanders ordered by Helen (*sic* but should be Mary) MacGregor to bind Bailie Nicol Jarvie and Frank Osbaldistone 'neck and heel' together, and throw them into a loch to seek their Highland kinfolk. Allan Ramsay (1684–1758), the poet born at Leadhills, is remembered chiefly for his *The Gentle Shepherd*, a realistic picture of Scottish life as he knew it. The famous Gorbals-born detective Allan Pinkerton (1819–84) emigrated to Chicago in 1843.

ALMA (f) Lat. *alma*, 'kind' or 'loving'. The name of several Roman goddesses. It occurs in Spenser's poem, *The Faerie Queen* (*c.* 1580), probably the finest poem written in England since Chaucer died in 1434, but was not widely used until after the Battle of Alma, during the Crimean War. *Alma Mater*, 'fostering mother', is used to denote the university at which a person has been educated.

ALPIN (m) Of uncertain origin and meaning, but presumably Gaelic, in which tongue it is rendered *Ailpein*.
Alpin, son of Eochaidh, a Pictish king, is on record
in 726. Alpin, son of Wroid, another Pict, reigned
775–80. The Scot, Alpin, possibly through marriage to
a Pictish princess, enabled his son Kenneth to unite the
Scots and Picts in 844. Alpin, a canon of Dunblane,
became bishop there in 1296. Alpin MacDonald witnessed a charter of the halfpenny land of the church of
Killian, granted to the monks of Paisley in 1295. The
surname MacAlpin, 'son of Alpin', is recorded as early
as 1260. Alpin has been used sparingly as a forename.
Alasdair Alpin MacGregor, a noted Scots author, died
in 1970.

ALTHEA (f) From the Gr. word meaning 'wholesome'.
The name was introduced in England with other classical names during the early Stewart period. Althea was
the name of the mother of Meleager, used by Richard
Lovelace (1618–58) in 'To Althea from Prison'. The
name is often confused with Alethia, 'good'. Neither
names have been fashionable in Scotland.

ALWYN (m) The name comes from Alvin, OE. *Aelfwine*,
'elf-friend', or *Aetheline*, 'noble friend'. Aldwine may
be an old variant, and a monk of this name was at
Jarrow as a contemporary of Turgot, Prior of Durham,
1087–1115. They were briefly at Melrose. Turgot
became Bishop of St Andrews and was the biographer of St Margaret of Scotland. Alwyn, Bishop of
Holyrood, resigned in 1150. Although never prolific in
Scotland, the name has been in regular use. The novel

Aylwin, by Theodore Watts-Dunton (1832–1914), helped to keep the name before the public. Alwin is a favoured variant, and the feminine form is Alwyne.

AMANDA (f) From the same root as AMABEL, meaning 'fit to be loved'. It was the name of several saints, and appeared in England early in the thirteenth century. At a later period it was favoured by playwrights and novelists. The name has gained in popularity since the Second World War (1939–45), and is now within the top thirty girls' names registered in Scotland. Pet forms are Mandie and Mandy. The French masculine form is Amand.

AMELIA (f) The feminine form of AEMILIUS, but has been largely superseded by EMILY. Amelia Ann Sophia, daughter of William, Lord Nairn in the Jacobite peerage, married about 1719, Laurence Oliphant of Gask. Amelia Murray (1763–1806), daughter of John, 3rd Duke of Atholl, married Capt. Thomas Ivie Cooke, Queen's American Rangers, as her first husband. The variant Emelia occurs in 1676 in the family of Murray of Glendoick. The Gaelic form is *Aimili*.

AMIE *See* AMY.

AMOS (m) From the Heb. word meaning 'carrier', or 'strong'. The Biblical Amos was a forester of Tekoa, who made an incursion into the public life of Israel, and was rejected, *c.* 750 BC. A shrewd observer of men and nature, he stopped little short of foretelling total destruction, and set a pattern for prophets who followed him (OT, Amos 1–12). The name came to be used in Scotland after the Reformation, but is now more often found as a surname. Amies and variants, found in England, is of different origin.

AMY (f) Fr. *amee*, feminine past participle of *amer* (modern *aimer*), 'to love'. A Latinised masculine form, Amatus, is found in early Christian inscriptions. Amy is now a very popular forename, being in the top ten girls' names registered in Scotland, and variants are Amia, AMIE, Aimee and Amey. The spelling Aimee is probably nearest the original. In Scott's *Kenilworth*, Amy Robsart is the tragic wife of the Earl of Leicester. Amy Johnson, died 1941, was a pioneer woman aviator, and first wife of another flyer, Glasgow-born Jim Mollison (1905–59).

ANABEL (f) Lat. *amabilis*, 'lovable'. The name has been in use since the twelfth century, but, except for a brief period in the nineteenth century, has given way to its short form, MABEL. George Augustus Frederick, 6th Earl Cowper, had daughters Florence Amabel (1840–86) and Amabel (1846–1906).

ANASTASIA (f) *See* STACEY, the abbreviated form.

ANDREW (m) Gr. and Lat. *Andreas*, 'manly'. In the scriptures Andrew, a fisherman of Bethsaids, and brother of PETER, is the first apostle. St Andrew is depicted in Christian art as an old man with long white hair, and leaning on a cross like the letter X, termed St Andrew's Cross. His day is 30 November. It is believed that he suffered martyrdom at Partrae in AD 70. His relics were brought to Scotland (in 761 according to Andrew Wyntoun) at a time, according to legend, when Hungus, son of Fergus the Pictish king, wintered in the Merse.

While walking with his seven earls, a voice purporting to be that of St Andrew promised him victory over his enemies if he dedicated the tenth part of his inheritance to God and the saint. The relics having arrived from Constantinople, he founded the town of St Andrews and died soon afterwards. The tradition of the St Andrews flag is supposed to have resulted from a cloud formation which gave representation of a white cross (X) against a blue background. Legend has it that this happened when Achius, King of Scots, and Hungus, King of the Picts, joined forces to oppose Athelstan, King of the West Saxons. The appearance of the cross so animated their forces that they killed Athelstan in East Lothian, at a place afterwards named Athelstaneford (pronounced locally as Elsinford). At any rate the emblem, Azure, a saltire Argent, was recognised as early as 1385, and recorded in Lyon Register pursuant to the act of 1672, as the national flag. Any Scot is entitled to fly the flag or wear a badge as evidence of his national patriotism or identity. The Gaelic form is *Aindrea*. Andrew, Archdeacon of Lothian, is recorded 1166–80, and Andrew, Bishop of Caithness, died in 1184. The name has always been a favourite in Scotland. Famous people who have borne the name include Sir Andrew Wood (1460–1540), a Scottish admiral, and Andrew Carnegie (1835–1919), who emigrated from Dunfermline to the USA and made a fortune in iron and steel. He became one of the world's greatest benefactors. Scott has Andrew as Ellangowan's old gardener in *Guy Mannering*, and as Ludovick Lesley's servant in *Quentin Durward*. Andrew first appears as a surname in the thirteenth century and gave rise to MacAndrew. Pet forms are Andy and Drew. The old feminine form Andrewina has given way to Andrina.

ANGEL (m,f) From the Gr. word for *angelos*, Lat. *angelus*, 'messenger, angel'. The name seems first borne by St Angelus, who travelled from Jerusalem to Sicily to preach the gospel early in the thirteenth century. He was assassinated. Angelo became a favourite name in Italy. Michael Angelo, the celebrated artist, lived 1474–1563. Angel appeared in England as a surname in the late twelfth century, sometimes rendered Angell, but was not much used as a forename before the early part of the seventeenth century. ANGELA is the most popular feminine form in Scotland today.

ANGELA (f) Has appeared as ANGEL, but now is recorded as Angela, with several variants: Angele, Angeline, Angelica and Angelique. Pet forms are Angie and Angy.

ANGUS (m) Gael. *aon-ghus*, 'unique choice'. The name is Latinised as Angusii, and in Gaeldom is rendered *Aonghus* or *Aonghais*. It is cognate with the Pictish *Hungus*. About 503 three brothers, sons of Erc, came from Dalriada in Ireland into territory (now Argyll and some adjacent islands) which they named after their former home. They were Fergus, Angus and Loarn. The *Cinel Aonghus* (clan of Angus) settled in Islay and Jura, but their descendants were driven out by the Danes about 850 and they settled in the mainland. Somerled, a direct descendant of the *Cinel Aonghus*, founded the Lordship of the Isles. The name is recorded at an early date in Ireland. St Angus, the Culdee, who died about 824, compiled a metrical calendar in which the saints of each day are commemorated in stanzas of four lines. The name was always popular in the Highlands and Western Islands, and appears also as a surname. Some people of the name derive it from the district of Angus, possibly from a hill to the east of Aberlemmo church. The 'Yerl' of Angus commands a regiment levied by the Covenanters, in Scott's *Old Mortality*. See also AENEAS. In 1864, Angus was fourteenth in popularity in Scotland, but has dropped outwith the top one hundred names. Gus is a popular pet name. The feminine form Augusina is seldom used today and is usually reduced to a pet form such as Angie or Sina.

ANITA (f) Spanish form of ANN. Nita is a pet form.

ANN, ANNA (f) Heb. 'grace', are really diminutive forms of Hanna or HANNAH, the name of the mother of the prophet Samuel (OT, 1 Samuel 1:1). The biblical Anna (NT, Luke 2:36) was a prophetess who spent her life serving God with prayer and fasting. Other Annas are Tobit's wife and the mother of the Virgin MARY. Anne, Annie, ANNETTE and Anita are variants. Anna (Helen Anne) Park, niece of Mrs Hyslop of the Globe Tavern in Dumfries, was Burns's 'Anna of the gowden locks'. She bore him an illegitimate daughter, Elizabeth (1791–1873), who married Pte John Thomson, of the Stirlingshire Militia, and they had a family whose names reflected her paternity. In Scott's *Count Robert of Paris*, Anna Comnena, princess, is the daughter of the Emperor Alexius and his wife Irene. Annot Lyle, in his *Legend of Montrose*, examples a diminutive. The Gaelic form for Ann is simply *Anna*, but appears frequently under the pet name Nannie.

ANNABEL, ANNABELLA (f) Probably from the Latin for 'lovable'. In early documents it is cognate with AMABLE but was used independently. Annabel, wife of Sir Patrick Graham (perhaps of Kincardine), signed the *Ragman Roll* in 1296. Annabella, the Latin form, has been popular in Scotland. Annabella, daughter of King James I and Joan Beaufort, married in 1447, Louis, Count of Geneva, but they were later divorced. She returned to Scotland and in 1459 married George, Earl of Huntly. Annabel Drummond was Queen Consort of Robert III, and the mother of James I. She is described in Scott's novel, *The Fair Maid of Perth*, as 'gifted with a depth of sagacity and firmness of mind'. Annaple is a peculiarly Scottish variant, and in Scott's story of *The Black Dwarf*, a woman of this name is Hobbie Elliot's old nurse. Other variant names are Anabel, Anabel, Anabill, Annable and Anabul. Pet forms are Bell and Bella.

ANNETTE (f) French form of ANN or Anne. The poet William W. Wordsworth had an illegitimate daughter Caroline by Annette Vallon, whom he met at Orléans in 1791. Had this not been for long concealed, he would never have become Poet Laureate in Victorian times.

ANTHONY (m) Lat., 'worthy of praise'. The name of a Roman *gens*, the most famous member of which was Mark Antony, the triumvir Marcus *Antonius*. He is a character in Shakespeare's *Julius Caesar* and in *Antony* and *Cleopatra*. Antony is historically correct, and the name was popular throughout Europe in the Middle Ages (Anton in Germany, Antonio in Italy and Antoine in France), probably due to the fame of St Antony the Great and St Antony of Padua. The spelling Anthony emerged after the Renaissance, when it was assumed to derive from the Gr. *anthos*, 'flower'. It is now the most favoured rendering. In Scott's *St Ronan's Well*, Anthony is the humped-backed position of Meg Dods. Tony is a short form, and the feminine form is ANTONIA. Anthony is also a surname, found in Angus and Fife early in the seventeenth century.

ANTONIA (f) Feminine form of ANTHONY, probably stemming from the French Antoinette. The best-known bearer of the name was Marie Antoinette, youngest daughter of the Empress Maria Theresa. She married Louis XVI of France in 1770 and was guillotined in 1793. Lady Antonia Fraser is a distinguished biographer. Short forms of the name are Toni, Toinette, Netta and Nettie.

APRIL (f) The name of the month much used as a forename since the First World War (1914–18) period. The variant AVRIL was popular for a time, but April has returned to fashion.

ARABELLA (f) Lat. *orabilis*, 'yielding to prayer'. The name was recorded in twelfth-century Scotland as *Orabilis*. Arabella Stuart died a prisoner in the tower of London in 1615. King James VII (1633–1701) had several natural children by Lady Arabella Churchill, sister of John, Duke of Malborough.

ARCHIBALD (m) O.G. *arch-bald*, 'bright bold'. Like some other compounds, the prefix does not qualify the second word, being two stems conjoined. It became the German *Ercanbold* and the Flemish *Erkinbald*. *Erkinbald*, probably descended from the Baldwins, Counts of Flanders, came to Scotland in the twelfth century, and married Eva, daughter of Paul O'Duine, the native Lord of Lochawe, from whom the Campbell chiefs descended. The name is curiously translated into Gaelic as Gillespic (*Gilleasbuig*), 'bishop's servant'. This is probably due to the mistaken notion that *bald*, in the original, meant 'hairless', and was equivalent to 'shaven one'. A brieve of William the Lion ordered Archibald and Hugh, sons of Swain of Forgan, to render the teind corn of Forgan to Scone Abbey. In many old documents Archibald is transliterated CELESTINE. Archibald appears also as a surname. Robert Archibald had a charter of the hospital of Roxburgh in 1390. In Scott's *Legend of Montrose*, Archibald, Earl of Argyll (afterwards Marquis) is referred to as 'Gillespie Grumach', the 'predominating influence in the West Highlands'. Variants of Archibald are Archbell and Archbold. Pet names are Arch, Archie, Archy and Baldy.

ARLINE (f) The name appears in Michael W. Balfe's opera, *The Bohemian Girl*, in 1843. The composer probably derived it from his wife, the Hungarian vocalist called Lina Rosa. Lina is a pet form of Karolina. The name is uncommon in Scotland, but some authorities associate it with the Gaelic *ol-air*, sometimes used for 'pledge'.

ARTHUR (m) Possibly of Irish origin, but disputed. The

name occurs among the northern and southern Cymry at the close of the sixth century and beginning of the seventh. Aedan mac Gabhrain, King of Scots, who died in 606, named a son Arthur, 'the first Gael', says Professor W.J. Watson, 'so far as we know, to bear that name'. His mother was a British princess. Arthur of Kincorth is recorded in 1435. The name appears also as a surname. John Airtheor was a juror at Duns in 1678. In Shetland the name emerged as a corrupt form of *Otho*. The name owes much to the legendary King Arthur, King of the Silures, whose wife, Guinever committed adultery with Lancelot of the Lake. The MacArthur clan were at the height of their power in the fourteenth century and appear to come from the same stock as the Campbells. The Gaelic form is Art or Artair. Arthur Conan Doyle (1859–1930), born in Edinburgh, was a prolific writer best known for his character Sherlock Holmes.

ASHLEIGH *See* Ashley.

ASHLEY (m) O.E., *aechleah*, 'ash wood'. This is a common English place-name which occurs over twenty times, and became a surname (e.g. The Earls of Shaftsbury). It began to be used as a forename in the 1860s. The character, Ashley Wilkes, in Margaret Mitchell's epic *Gone with the Wind*, has probably favoured Ashley. ASHLEIGH is also in use. Lee is a short form, sometimes used independently.

ATHOL, ATHOLL (m) A territorial name, used as a surname and sparingly as a forename. Gilbert and Thomas Atholl, white fishers, were at Footdee, Aberdeen, in

1592, and were admitted burgesses of Aberdeen in 1606. Atholl Monson Forbes (1841–1953), was 20th Baron Forbes, and his son, Atholl Laurence Cunyingham Forbes (1882–1953), 21st Baron. Athol L. Murray was Keeper of the Records of Scotland, 1985–90.

AUDREY (f) A short form of the now obsolete O.E. *Etheldreda*, which now appears in another short form, ETHEL, St Audrey is mentioned by Bede (673–735), and she died of a tumour in her throat, which she regarded as punishment for her early love of necklaces. At St Audrey's Fair, necklaces were sold, but they were not of good quality – the word 'tawdry' evolved from these. The name was in general use from the sixteenth century by country folk, and although still in use in Scotland, it has never been prolific.

AUGUSTA (f) Feminine form of AUGUSTUS. It was introduced to England by Augusta of Saxe-Gotha, wife of Frederick, Prince of Wales, and the mother of George III. A daughter was named Augusta Sophia. Augusta, daughter of George (Mackenzie), 3rd Earl of Cromartie, married in 1770, Sir William Murray of Ochtertyre, Bart. The name is not now fashionable.

AUGUSTUS (m) Lat., 'venerable'. Augustus was adopted as a second name by some of the German princes after the Renaissance, and became an ordinary forename. It was brought to England by the Hanoverians, and was popular in the nineteenth century. Auguste is common in France and August in Germany. The full Latin form, Augustine, was often shortened to AUSTIN. Anne, *suo jure* Countess of Orkney, married in 1720 her cousin,

William (O'Brien), 4th Earl of Inchiquin, and had a son Augustus, Lord O'Brien. Like ANGUS, the usual pet form is Gus, but occasionally Gussie is used.

AULAY (m) Two names of different origin, but both Gael., appear alike in English form. The first is from the personal name *Amhalghaidh*, pronounced almost as Owlay or Aulay. From this came the Aulay of the old earls of Lennox and the Dumbartonshire MacAulays. Sir Aulay MacAulay of Ardincaple is included in a roll of landlords and bailies, 1587. The second derivation, *MacAmhlaibh* or *MacAmhlaidh* 'son of Amlaib', gave the Hebridean name (Gael. form of the Norse *Olafr*) Macaulay. Thomas B. MacAulay (1800–59), the eminent historian, was of Hebridean descent. Although not prolific the forename Aulay is still in use.

AURORA (f) Gr. *Eos*, a daughter of Hyperion, was one of the Titans and goddess of the dawn. The name was introduced into Britain in the sixteenth century from Central Europe. *Aurora Leigh* is a romance in blank verse by Elizabeth Barrett Browning (1856), in which the heroine is so named, and tells the story of her life. In Byron's *Don Juan* 'Aurora Raby' is a beautiful and innocent young heiress. The name is uncommon in Scotland. See also DAWN.

AUSTIN (m) A popular diminutive of Augustine, derived from the Latin AUGUSTUS. It is in current use, but not in the top one hundred boys' names registered in Scotland. Austin is also a surname which appears in the fourteenth century and is occasionally derived from Uisdean (*Huisdean*), rendered HUGH in many cases.

AVRIL (f) Fr. 'April'. The name has been in use for about a century: rather more in Scotland than in England, but has given way to APRIL.

B

BALDWIN (m) O.G. *bald-win*, 'bold friend'. Baldwin of Biggar came from Devonshire about the middle of the twelfth century and became Sheriff of Lanark. He built a motte at Boghall, near Biggar, *c.* 1170. Another Baldwin, a harness-maker, seems to have come direct from Flanders at the invitation of David I (1124–53), to settle at Perth. The name did not become prolific in Scotland, but had variant spellings such as Baldene, Baldon and Baldonye, which appear as surnames in the sixteenth century. The name was more common in England, where resulting surnames are Bodkin and Bowden.

BARBARA (f) From a Gr. word meaning 'strange' or 'foreign'. At first the name probably meant anyone who did not speak the language, but in early Christian times Barbara was favoured as a name for girls. St Barbara was martyred in the third century and was venerated in the Middle Ages. The name went out of favour during the Reformation, but not entirely out of use. James Sandelands of Cruvie and his wife Catherine Scot, married in 1556/7, had a daughter Barbara. Lady Barbara

Ruthven was one of Queen Anne's maids of honour in 1600, at the time of the Gowrie Conspiracy. The name made a recovery at the beginning of the present century, but is not now within the top one hundred girls' names. Short forms are Babs and Baubie.

BARRY (m) Gael. *bearrach*, 'spear'. Probably of Irish origin, and appears there also as a surname. Cavin Barry was one of their martyrs, celebrated in a nationalist song. Scotland's famous playwright and novelist, James M. Barrie (1860–1937), was a native of Kirriemuir.

BARTHOLOMEW (m) From a Heb. or Aramaic word meaning 'son of Talmai', ('abounding in furrows'). It was the patronymic of the apostle NATHANIEL, by which name he is commonly known. The name appears both as forename and surname, and in respect of the latter has given us variants such at Bates, Bartle, Bateson, Batts and Batson, mainly in England. Short forms are Bat, Bart and Bartie. Bartholomew (called Berty) Wardlaw, bowmaker in Edinburgh, was paid 24s. for arrows made for the king in 1497. Sir David Home of Wedderburn, killed at Flodden in 1513, left a son Bartholomew. Bartholomew is rendered *Parlan* in Gaelic, and the MacFarlane chiefs descended from Bartholomew, who lived in the reign of David II. The name has been said to mean 'brotherly', and Scott, in his *Anne of Geierstein*, makes Bartholomew, 'a poor lay brother', guide to English merchants on the first stage of their journey from La Ferette to Strasburg. A Bartholomew family farmed in the vicinity of Broxburn and Winchburgh for a long period.

BASIL (m) From a Gr. word meaning 'kingly'. The name appears in early Christian inscriptions. St Basil the Great, Bishop of Caesarea, who died in AD 379, defended the church against heresy. Basil I was the Macedonian Byzantine emperor 867–886. The name has been in use since the twelfth century. Basil William Douglas-Hamilton, Lord Daer (1763–94), met the poet Burns at Catrine in 1786. The distinguished architect, Sir Basil Urwin Spence (1907–76), designer of Coventry Cathedral, was born in India of Scottish parents. Old, but seldom used, feminine forms are Basilia and Basilie. The name has resulted in the surnames Bassill, Bazell, Basely, and Bazley.

BEATRICE, BEATRIX (f) Lat. *beatricem*, 'bringer of joy'. The name of a fourth-century Roman saint, which spread to Celtic Ireland and Scotland. Malcolm I, King of Scots, had a daughter Beatrice, the mother of Duncan, who succeeded his grandfather in 1034. In 1039 he was assassinated by MacBeth (possibly a cousin), whose wife Gruach was the Lady MacBeth of Shakespeare. Beatrix was the most common spelling in early times. Somerled of the Isles, killed in 1164, had a daughter so named, who was Prioress of Iona. Beatrice, daughter of Robert de Brus, 'the noble', ancestor of King Robert I, was in 1221 the wife of Hugo de Neville. The name remained popular, and from *c*. 1548 was much favoured by the Campbells of Breadalbane. In Scott's *Castle Dangerous*, Sister Beatrice, of St Bride's Convent, was 'blessed with a winning gift of making comfits and syllabubs'. Pet forms of the name are

Bee and Trixie. The name has gone out of fashion in Scotland.

BELINDA (f) The name is of uncertain origin, but may contain the O.G. element, *lindi*, meaning 'serpent', esteemed for wisdom. The name was used by Pope in *The Rape of the Lock* (1712). Since then it has been associated with the Spanish *linda*, 'pretty'. Billinda has been recorded, but for a girl whose father was William (Bill). Pet forms are Lyn, Lynn, Lynne, Lyndi and Lynnda. See also LINDA.

BENJAMIN (m) In Heb. interpreted as 'son of the right hand'. In the scriptures Benjamin was the youngest of the twelve sons of Jacob. His mother was RACHEL, who died giving birth to him. At first he was called Benoni, 'son of my sorrow', but his father called him Benjamin (OT, Genesis 35:18) and his children were Benjamites. The name was common after the Reformation and much favoured by Jewish families. Benjamin, son and heir apparent of Sir William Dunbar of Hempriggs, 1st Baronet (1706), married Janet Sinclair, but died in his father's lifetime, without issue. Benjamin Franklin (1706–90), scientist, printer and bookseller, gave the name prominence in America. The first of a long line of Scottish medical men in the Bell family was Benjamin (1749–1806), who was a surgeon in Edinburgh. In Scott's *Redgauntlet*, Benji Coltherd appears as an 'impudent urchin'. The Gaelic form of the name is *Beathan*. Short forms are Ben (sometimes used independently), Benji and Benny. Benna has been recorded as a feminine form.

BERNADETTE (f) Derived from the French diminutive for BERNARD, and has gained currency from St Bernadette Soubirous (1844–79) of Lourdes. The name is outwith the top hundred girls' names, but favoured in Scotland (and in Ireland) by Catholic families.

BERNARD (m) O.G. *berin*, 'bear', and *hard*, 'stern'. The cognate O.E. form was *Beornheard*, the first element having acquired the sense 'brave', or 'noble'. It came to Britain after the Conquest. Bernardo *filius* Tocce witnessed a grant by Thor to the Abbey of Holyrood *c.* 1150. Bernard de Linton, Abbot of Arbroath, became Bishop of the Isles in 1328. The name became popular in Scotland and Ireland, especially among Catholic families. *Bearnard* is the Gaelic form. Bernie and Barney are short forms, and the feminine form is BERNADETTE.

BERNICE (f) Gr., properly *Berenice*, 'bringer of victory'. The name was spread by the conquests of Alexander the Great, and became popular in Egypt. Bernice, daughter of Herod Agrippa I, King of Judea, AD 37–44, rounded off a series of marriages and a bout of incest with her brother Agrippa II by becoming mistress of the future Emperor Titus, but he was forced by her unpopularity at Rome to get rid of her. Racine portrayed her as a tragic heroine, which is probably more than she deserved. The name began to be used in England after the Reformation, but it has not enjoyed wide use in Scotland.

BERTHA (f) O.G., *Berahta*, the name of a female deity, from *beraht*, 'bright'. The earliest notable Bertha

(Bercta) was the wife of Etherbert, King of Kent (died 616) grandson of Hengist, the Saxon conqueror. She was a Frankish princess. Charlemange (742–814), King of the Franks, had a daughter Berta, who married the poet-courtier, Angilbert de Ponthieu. The name was in regular use throughout the Middle Ages, and after a period of decline came back into use in the nineteenth century.

BERTRAM (m) Lat. compound *berhta*, 'bright', and *hraben*, 'raven', giving 'shining raven'. The name appears with variant spellings all over Europe. Bertram, son of Adam of Lesser Riston, sold to the Prior of Coldingham in the twelfth century, Turkil Hog, a serf, along with his son and daughters. The name appears more frequently as a surname. Johan Bertram, burgess of Inverkeithing, rendered homage in 1296. Walter Bertrahame, Provost of Edinburgh, was ambassador to France in 1482. Probably the name is best known through Bertram Mills, the circus owner. Short forms are Bert, Bertie, and occasionally Berry, which is a surname of independent origin.

BETHIA (f) Heb. *bith-yah*, 'daughter (i.e. worshipper) of *Jehovah*'. Bithia was the name of a daughter of Pharaoh and his wife Mered (OT, 1 Chronicles 4:4). Bethia appears as a Christian name in Scotland from the sixteenth century. Bethia, daughter of William Maule, merchant-burgess of Edinburgh (1579), and his wife Bethia Guthrie, married James Murray of Skirling in 1601. Bethia is a variant spelling, and the name shares the short form Beth with ELIZABETH.

BETSY (f) Although a pet name for ELIZABETH, the name is often used independently. The Gaelic form is *Beitidh*.

BETTY (f) A short form of ELIZABETH, like BETSY, this name is frequently used independently. Walter MacFarlane (1698–1767), clan chief and antiquary, married in 1760 Lady Betty Erskine, who was thirty-five years his junior. Robert Laidlaw in Hopehouse, a maternal uncle of James Hogg, the Ettrick Shepherd, married Betty Biggar (1741–1820).

BEVERLY, BEVERLEY (m, f) O.E., 'of the beaver-meadow'. The name appears as a male surname in England about the end of the nineteenth century. Beverley Nichols (1898–1983) was a well-known novelist and composer. The name is used in Scotland mainly for girls.

BILL (m) Short form of WILLIAM. As Billy it appears as an independent name. Billinda has been recorded as a female form. 'The Bill' is a slang expression for the police and the name of a popular TV series.

BLAIR (m, f) A Scottish surname of territorial origin, recorded early in the twelfth century. It now appears regularly as a forename and is within the top eighty names recorded annually. In the USA it has appeared as a female name.

BRENDA (f) O.Nor. *brandr*, from 'brand' or 'sword'. The name was common in the Shetland Isles and spread probably through Sir Walter Scott's use of it in *The Pirate*, in which Magnus Troil's youngest daughter is so named. In Ireland it is regarded as a feminine form of BRENDAN, but this may be a fairly modern explanation.

BRENDAN (m) Gael., possible a compound of *breun*, 'filthy', and *find*, 'hair'. Brendan Mocualti, son of Finnlogh, was an Irish holy man, who founded the church of Clonfert and became known as St Brendan. Another Brendan, a contemporary who died in 573, was son of Neman, and called St Brendan of Birr. The name came late to Scotland, but is not uncommon in families of Irish descent.

BRIAN (m) Of doubtful origin, but the *bre* element may mean 'hill'. The name has long been popular in Ireland because of the national hero, Brian Boroimhe, but is found also in England in the Middle Ages, probably imported from Brittany. It reached Scotland in the reign of William the Lion (1165–1214), during whose reign Linaldus *filius* Brian is mentioned, and also Bernard *filius* Brien, who gave a carucate in Hauden to the Abbey of Kelso. The name came into use as a surname early in the fifteenth century and variants are Bryan, Bryand and Bryane. Brian and Brianne are currently in use as Christian names.

BRIDGET (f) Gael., derived from a Celtic fire goddess and from a fifth-century Irish saint. It can also come from the O.Fr. *Brigitte* made famous by the actress Brigitte Bardot (Camile Javel, born 1934). The cult of St Brighid was popular in Ireland, where the spelling Bridget is common, and in England, where Bride and Bryde have been used. The name may have been used in England before it became prolific in Ireland. George Hamilton, son of James, Baron of Mountcastle and Viscount of Strabane, had a daughter Bridget, who died a widow in 1789. Bridget Douglas (1758–1842), daughter of James, 13th Earl of Morton, married William, 1st Earl of Radnor. Variant forms are Brigid and Bedelia, and pet names are Beesy and Biddy, the last often a general nickname for an Irish woman.

BRUCE (m) A surname of Norman extraction, famous in Scottish history. It was a favourite name for the Bruce Earls of Carrick, and Earl Robert Bruce became King of Scots in 1306. His famous victory over the English at Bannockburn established the independence of Scotland. The use as a forename probably dates from early in the eighteenth century. Bruce Campbell (1734–1813) was owner of the estate of Mayfield, Galston in Ayrshire. The name is in current use, but outwith the top one hundred boys' names.

BRYAN *See* BRIAN

C

CADWALLADER (m) A Welsh compound name, *cad*, 'battle', and *gwaladr*, 'leader', giving 'battle chief'. Cadwalla was king of the West Britons and he rebelled against Edwin, king of Northumbria, in 683. Cadwallader Colden (1688–1776), born in Ireland, emigrated from

Oxnam, Berwickshire, where his father was parish minister, to Philadelphia, Pennsylvania, and became Lt Governor of New York. Cadwallader has also appeared as a surname.

CAITLIN (f) An Irish form of Kathleen, ultimately Catherine; rendered CATRIONA in the Gaelic of Scotland. The name is becoming more common, and is now within the top one hundred girls' names registered annually.

CALLUM (m) A diminutive form of MALCOLM, with variants Calum and Cailean.

CALVIN (m) Lat. *Calvinus*, from *calvus*, 'bald'. The name of a Roman clan, and first used as a forename in honour of John Calvin (1509–64), the Swiss Protestant reformer. The name, while in current use in Scotland, is more popular in the USA, where Calvin Coollidge was President, 1923–29.

CAMERON (m) A surname that is used as a Christian name. It is of both Highland and Lowland origin. The Lowland name derives from three places: Cameron on the outskirts of Edinburgh, Cameron in the Lennox and Cameron in Fife. The Highland name probably comes from a nickname stemming from a facial deformity; *cam-shron*, for 'wry' or 'hook nose'. Examples of both are found in the fifteenth century, and of course Cameron is a famous clan associated with Lochaber. Use as a forename began in Scotland, and examples are known where children have been so named after a minister on the occasion of his first baptism in a new charge.

CAMILLA (f) Lat., but of obscure origin. Camilla was the virgin queen of the Volscians. Virgil (*Aeneid*, vii, 809) says she was so swift that she could make her way over the sea without wetting her feet. Fanny Burney (Madame D'Arblay, 1752–1840) wrote a novel called *Camilla* (1796). The name has been in regular, if not widespread, use but has recently declined in popularity, possibly through association with Mrs Camilla Parker Bowles' relationship with the heir to the throne of Britain. The French form, Camille, is also in current use.

CAMPBELL (m) Another surname which is occasionally used as a Christian name. Col. Campbell Dalrymple (1725–99) of Carriden, was a son of David Dalrymple, a Lord of Session.

CANDACE, CANDICE (f) The origin of this name is unknown but appears to have been a dynastic name for the queens of Ethiopia, one of whom owned a eunuch who had charge of her treasure. He was converted to Christianity and baptised by the deacon PHILIP (NT, Acts 8:27–38). Candice or Candace came to be used as a forename. Candace Stevenson, winner of the 1949 Poetry Society of America award, and the actress Candice Bergen probably influenced usage in America. The name is in current, but not wide use in Scotland. Pet forms are Candi and Candy.

CARLY (f) A pet name for CAROLINE, now used independently.

CAROL (f) A short form of CAROLINE, now often recorded as a name in its own right. In fact it is now more popular in Scotland than the parent name. Carol is occasionally used as a male name, also the German form Karl, as well as Carl and Carlo.

CAROLINE, CAROLINA (f) The name derives from *Carolina*, the Italian form of CHARLES. King George III, who reigned 1727–60, married Caroline of Anspach in 1705, and the name became popular. Lady Caroline Campbell, eldest daughter of John, 2nd Duke of Argyll, married Frances, Earl of Dalkeith, in 1742. The noted song-writer, Baroness Caroline Nairne (1766–1845), was a daughter of the Jacobite laird, Oliphant of Gask. CAROL, Carola and Carolyn are now variants, and pet names are Carrie, Carly, Caddy and Lina. In a few cases the name is derived from the American state.

CATHARINE, CATHERINE (f) *See* KATHARINE/KATHERINE. A 'Catherine Wheel' is a spoked window or window compartment, a rotating firework, or a lateral somersault. The term derives from the spiked wheel which was the instrument of St Catherine's martyrdom. Catherine Glover, 'a most beautiful young woman', appears in Scott's novel *The Fair Maid of Perth*. Pet forms of the name are Cath and Cathie (*see also* KATHARINE).

CATRIONA (f) The Gaelic form of CATHERINE/KATHERINE. This is the title of a book by R.L. Stevenson, and it helped to make the name popular.

CECIL (m) Lat., *Caecilius*, probably derived from *caecus*, 'blind'. The name and its feminine form, CECILIA, appear on Christian inscriptions of the Roman Empire. It came to England at the Norman Conquest, and appears as Saycell, Seisel, Seysel, Cecill and Seisill, but curiously was less in use than the feminine form which occasionally was used for boys. Robert Hamilton of Presmennan, WS, named a daughter Cecil in 1676. The name become more general from the fame of Cecil John Rhodes (1853–1902), imperialist and benefactor, but is not prolific in Scotland.

CECILIA (f) Feminine form of CECIL. St Cecilia was a Roman lady who underwent martyrdom in the third century and became the patron saint of music and of the blind. The name appears in England early in the twelfth century, when Cecilia de Romelie, heiress of Skipton, married William Meschin, Lord of Copeland. Their daughter Alice married before 1140, William Fitz Duncan, a Scottish military man, and they had a daughter Cecilia. Devorgille, wife of John Balliol, had a daughter Cecilia, mentioned in a charter of 1273. The name was much favoured by the family Wemyss of Wemyss in the sixteenth and seventeenth centuries. *Sile*, or *Silis*, the Irish form of the name, gave rise to SHEILA, a popular name in Scotland. Variant spellings are Celia, Cecily, Cicily and Cicilly. *Sia* is an Irish abbreviation, and Sis or Sissy are pet names.

CELESTE (†) Lat. *caelestis*, 'heavenly'. The variant CELESTINE has been recorded for males and females.

CELESTINE (m, f) The name was a transliteration of the Gaelic *Gilleasbuig* or ARCHIBALD. It was known anciently among the MacDonalds. Celestine, Gillespic or Archibald of Lochalsh, son of Alexander MacDonald, received the lands of Lochalsh and Lochcarron in 1457. *See also* CELESTE.

CHANTEL (f) Derived from a French word meaning 'stony place'. It came into use in honour of St Jeanne of Chantal (1572–1641). Importation of the name in modern times had led to variant spellings such as Chanelle, Chantelle and Shantell.

CHARITY (f) Lat. 'Christian love'. The Puritans became accustomed to name each child after one of the virtues. Faith, Hope and Charity, were names often given to triplets. Wider use of the name probably stemmed from Bunyan's *Pilgrim's Progress*. Dickens, in *Martin Chuzzlewit*, shortened the name to CHERRY, a name now more popular than Charity.

CHARLES (m) O.G. *ceorl*, 'man'. Lat. *Carolus*, and adapted by the French to Charles. The name was very popular in the Middle Ages due to the fame of the Emperor Charles the Great, called Charlemange (742–814). It was used by subsequent French and German emperors, also by the Spanish and Swedish royal families. The Normans brought the name to Britain, but it was used sparingly until taken up by the House of Stewart in the seventeenth century. It proved an ill-omened name for kings. Charles I was beheaded, Charles II lived long in exile, and Charles Edward, the 'Young Pretender', died in reduced circumstances. In spite of those dismal facts the name remained in favour. In 1864 it was the tenth most popular name for boys, but has dropped to just inside the top ninety names. Variants are Charlie and Carlo, and the usual feminine form is CHARLOTTE. In modern Gaelic Charles is rendered *Tearlach*, derived from *Teardhealbach* 'well shaped'.

CHARLOTTE (f) A French feminine form of CHARLES (*see also* CAROLINE). It came to Britain early in the seventeenth century and became well established. Charles II had a natural daughter Charlotta, born *c.* 1650. Charlotte Murray, daughter of James, 2nd Duke of Atholl, was born in 1731. The most powerful influence was the marriage in 1761, of Charlotte Sophia of Mecklenburgh-Strelitz to King George III. Charlotte Stuart, Duchess of Albany, legitimated in 1784, was the daughter of Prince Charles Edward and his mistress, Clementina Walkinshaw. The poet Burns met Charlotte Hamilton (1763–1806), half sister of his friend GAVIN Hamilton, at Harvieston, near Dollar, in 1787, and celebrated her beauty in 'The Banks of Devon'. Charlene is a modern variant, and short forms of Charlotte are Charlie, Chatty, Lottie, Lotty and Tottie.

CHELSEA (f) From the London place-name meaning 'landing place for chalk or limestone'. The forename was possibly first used in Australia, where there is a place named after the London one. The name is in current use in Scotland, and variants are Chelsey and Chelsie. Chelsea was the name of a character played by Jane Fonda in the film *On Golden Pond*.

CHERIE (f) Fr. 'dear one'. Variants are Sheryl, Sheree, Sheri, Sherie and Sherry.

CHERRY (f) A pet form of CHARITY. Cher is a pet form.

CHLOE (f) Gr. 'green shoot'. A name given to the Goddess Demeter, who protected the green fields. Chloe is mentioned in the scriptures (NT, 1 Corinthians 1:11) by St Paul, and in classical literature it was a pastoral named echoed by Elizabethan poets. The name is well used in Scotland today.

CHRISTABEL (f) Lat. 'beautiful Christian', a compound of *Christ* and *bella*, 'fair'. The name was first used in Britain in the sixteenth century, but has mainly been a literary name. Thomas Percy (1729–1811) used it in his 'Ballad of Sire Cauline'. Possibly Samuel T. Coleridge (1772–1834) made use of this source when penning his poem 'Christabel'. Variant spellings include Christabella, Christabelle and Christella. Pet forms are Chris, Christie and Chrissie.

CHRISTIAN (m, f) Lat. *Christianus*, from the Gr. *Christos*, 'anointed'. It was mainly used as a female name in the Middle Ages, but occasionally appears as masculine. Its use probably spread after the publication of John Bunyan's *Pilgrim's Progress* in 1684. In that curious work Christian and Christiana his wife are the main protagonists. However, the name was previously well used in Scotland. Christian, sister of King Robert Bruce, married Andrew de Moravia. Christiana, daughter of Colin Campbell of Lochawe, married Duncan MacFarlane of Arrochar, *c.* 1395. Scott has used the name in *Peveril of the Peak*. In modern times Christiaan N. Barnard, the South African surgeon, pioneered heart transplanting. Variant feminine forms are Christina, Kristina, Chrissie and Christy. Pet names for Christine are Tenny and Tina. The Gaelic form of Christian is *Cairistine* or *Cairistiana*.

CHRISTOPHER (m) Lat. *Christopherus*, 'one who carries Christ in his heart'. This interpretation led to the story of St Christopher (patron saint of travellers) carrying the child Christ across a river. The name has fluctuated in popularity. In Scotland the name was often rendered as Chrystal or Crystal. This form appears in Barbour's *Bruce*, in the story of the rescue at Methven in 1306 of the newly crowned king from Philip de Moubray, by Christopher de Seton. Nearer our own time Christopher Murray Grieve (1892–1978), writing as Hugh McDiarmid, emerged as one of Scotland's most influential literary men. Christopher is a very popular forename today, and variants recorded in recent years are KRISTIAN, KRISTOFER, Kristoffer and Kristopher. Pet forms are Chris, Christie, Kit and Kris. Christopher is rendered *Gillecroisd* (Gilchrist) in Gaelic.

CIARAN (m) Gael. *ciar*, 'dusky'. An old surname now coming into use as a Christian name. The *Clann Chiaran* was attached to the Grants, and their original homeland was Dallachaple, in Cromdale. The surname is cognate with Macilheran, an old Bute name which emerged as Sharp. The Irish *Keiran* has the same meaning, but evolved independently.

CINDY *See* CYNTHIA.

CLAIRE (f) French form of CLARE, and now more popular.

CLARA, CLARE (f) Lat. *clarus*, 'bright', 'clear'. The Italian order of the Sisters of St Clare, or *Poor Clares*, founded in the thirteenth century, made the name popular throughout Europe. John Leslie of Wardis and his fifth wife had a daughter, Clara, who married Patrick Leith of Harthill before 1532. The usual English spelling was

CLARE. Variants are CLAIRE, Claribel, CLARINDA and Clarice, an Italian form, and Clarissa. Clarie is a pet name. The Gaelic form of Clare is *Sorcha*.

CLARENCE (m) Derives from the Dukedom created in 1362 for the English King Edward III's son Lionel, who had married the heiress of Clare, in Suffolk. The title was revived in 1789 for the future William IV, and again in 1890 for Albert Victor, son of Edward VII. Clarence has been used as a forename in many parts of the world, but is not much used in Scotland. CLARE is not a feminine form, but a name in its own right.

CLARINDA (f) A diminutive form of CLARE. It was popular in the eighteenth century and used to some extent in the nineteenth. The poet Burns, as *Sylvander*, carried on a correspondence with Mrs Agnes (or Nancy) McLehose, residing in Edinburgh, in which she was *Clarinda*. The affair prompted 'Ae fond kiss', considered by Sir Walter Scott to be 'the essence of a thousand love tales'.

CLAUD (m) Lat. *claudus*, 'lame'. The name of two Roman clans, one patrician, the other plebeian. The name came to be much used in France as Claude. In Scotland the name was regularly used by the Hamiltons. Lord Claud Hamilton, fourth son of James, 2nd Earl of Arran, born *c.* 1543, was progenitor of the Earls of Abercorn. Claud, a younger son of Robert Dalzell of that Ilk, died in 1597. The name is now uncommon. Claudian is a variant, and Claudie has been recorded as a pet form. See also CLAUDIA.

CLAUDIA (f) Feminine form of CLAUD. Claudia Schiffer is a famous 'supermodel'.

CLEMENT (m) Lt. *clemens*, 'mild', or perhaps 'merciful'. The name of a saint commemorated in many church dedications; also the name of several popes. It was well used before the Reformation, but faded until Victorian times, when it staged a revival. However, it is not much used today, except as a surname. *See also* CLEMENTINE.

CLEMENTINE (f) Feminine form of CLEMENT, made famous by the song 'My Darling Clementine', also by a classic western film which starred the late Henry Fonda. James Francis Edward Stuart, known as The Old Pretender (to the British crown), married in 1719, Clementine, daughter of Prince James Sobieski, son of John, King of Poland. They were the parents of 'Bonnie Prince Charlie', who attempted to regain the British throne in 1745. Some Jacobite families used the name, doubly meaningful as it was the name of the prince's mistress, Clementine Walkingshaw, who bore him a daughter Charlotte. Lady Clementine Fleming, daughter of John, 6th Earl of Wigtown, married in 1735, Charles, 10th Lord Elphinston. Their daughter Clementina (1749–1822) married James Drummond, Lord Perth and they too had a daughter Clementine. Clementine, wife of Sir Winston Churchill (1874–1965), was of Scottish descent, a daughter of Col Henry Montague Hozier, of the family Hozier of Mauldslie, Lanarkshire. The name is uncommon today. Pet forms are Clem, Clemmie and Tina.

COLIN (m) Gael., *cailean*, 'a youth'. The name has always been common in Scotland and Ireland, especially in

Gaelic-speaking areas. Sir Colin Campbell, called 'Mor' or 'big', who died about 1296, gave his name to the Campbell chiefs, whose patronymic is *MacCalean Mor*. The name Colin has been popular among many branches of the clan, and surnames derived from it include Colinson, Colins and Collins. The Christian name is within the top fifty boys names registered annually in Scotland. Feminine forms are Colina and Collette, and in some cases Colleen.

Colina (f) Feminine form of Colin. Colina, daughter of Colin Campbell, heir apparent of Sir James Campbell of Aberuchill and Catharine Fraser, married Thomas Hogg, merchant-burgess of Edinburgh, in 1757. The name is not now prolific.

Collette, Collette (f) French diminutive of Nicole, or rather Nicolette, feminine form of Nicholas. Variants are Coletta and Colleta.

Conan (m) Gael., derived from *conan*, 'high'. The name was introduced to Ireland after the Norman Conquest and may stem from a Celtic word. Among several saints of the name, one was progenitor of the Dukes of Brittany. In Irish legend Conan is represented as a kind of Thersites, brave and daring, even to rashness. The best-known bearer of the name in Scotland was Edinburgh-born Sir Arthur Conan Doyle (1859–1930), creator of the fictional detective, Sherlock Holmes. The name is in regular use, and the surnames Conan, Connart, Connand, Conon and Conning derive from it. The film *Conan the Barbarian* (1982) starred Arnold Schwarzenegger.

CONNOR (m) Gael., Irish *concobhar*, 'high desire'. The name is found in Ireland as Connaire, and figures in Irish mythology. Conor Mac Nessa was king of Ulster in the first century AD. It is now within the top one hundred boys' names in Scotland and appears also as a surname. Conor Cruise O'Brien, born 1917, is a leading Dublin journalist and author.

CONSTANCE (f) Lat. *constantia*, 'steadfast' or 'constant'. The name became popular in Christendom after Constantine the Great ordered toleration in AD 313. Constance, sister of Conan, Duke of Brittany and Earl of Richmond, by Margaret, daughter of Malcolm IV, was once considered as a bride for the latter, but married Alain of Rohan, *c*. 1165. The name came to England at the Conquest, and it appears as Custance in Chaucer's 'The Man of Law's Tale'. Constantia also appears, and Connie is the usual short form. Constance, daughter of Sir Walter Alston (created Baron of Forfar in 1627), married in 1629, Walter Fowler. The name, despite D.H. Lawrence's raunchy heroine, Lady Constance Chatterley, has remained in regular, but not wide use.

CONSTANTINE (m) Lat. as for CONSTANCE. Constantine, Emperor of Rome, took part in an expedition against the Picts before AD 306. Three other emperors bore the name. The Scots of Dalriada had three kings named Constantine between 862 and 997, and there was a Pictish king of the name, 789–820. It has been suggested that Constantine, 2nd Earl of Fife, was of regal origin, and given the dignity in succession to Ethelred, third son of Malcolm Canmore and Queen Margaret, *c*. 1107. The name appears also in the genealogy of the ancient Earls of Atholl. Constantin was Abbot of Newbattle, 1233–36. The name was not popular in later centuries, but the feminine form, CONSTANCE, has remained in regular use.

CORA (f) Gr., from the word for 'maiden'. The name appeared in Britain after the publication in 1826, of James Fennimore Cooper's novel, *The Last of the Mohicans*. CORAL is sometimes a variant, but Cora has largely given way to CORINNE and Coralie.

CORDELIA (f) This rather scarce name first appeared as Cordeilla in the sixteenth century in Holinshed's *Chronicle*. Shakespeare altered it to Cordelia for his play *King Lear*. The name is probably the same as Cordula, who appears in Welsh and Cornish calendars as a companion of St Ursula. Cordelia Harvey was buried at St Martin's in the Field, in 1636. Cordelia, born 1712, daughter of Sir George Wishart of Cliftonhall, Midlothian, married William Sinclair of Roslyn. The name has gone out of fashion.

CORINNE, CORINNA (f) Gr., a diminutive of the word for 'girl' or maiden' (See CORA). It was given to the Goddess *Persephone*, associated with the coming of spring. The Greek poetess who bore the name in the fifth century may have inspired later poets, especially Robert Herrick (1591–1674). Corinna and Corinne are in use in Scotland today. *See also* CORA.

CORMAC (m) Gael. *corb-mac*, 'charioteer'. An old personal name mentioned by Adamnan, and now found in the surname MacCormaig or MacCormack, 'son of Cormac'.

CORNELIUS (m) Lat. *cornu*, 'horn'. The horn was symbolic of kinship in Roman culture, and Cornelius was a famous clan name. In the scriptures, Cornelius was a centurian who, in obedience to a dream, sent to Joppa for Simon Peter to preach at Caesarea (NT, Acts 10:1–22). The name has never been prolific in Scotland. Cornelius Crawford of Jordanhill was served heir to Hew, his father, in 1625. His great grandson, the Rev. Cornelius Crawford, was rector of Mursly, in Buckinghamshire. Short forms are Corney, Corny, Cornie and Corrie. Cornelia has been recorded as a feminine form.

COSMO (m) Gr., from the word meaning 'order'. Cosmo was the name of one of the patron saints of Milan, and was used by the Italian family of Medici in the form of Cosimo from the fourteenth century onwards. Cosmo George (1710–1800), was named in honour of Cosimo de Medici III, Grand Duke of Tuscany, who was a friend of his father. Cosmo Innes (1798–1874), Professor of Constitutional Law at Edinburgh, was an eminent historian. The name is now uncommon.

COSPATRIC (m) Derived from *givas*, 'young servant of Patrick'. The name appears in the eleventh century as Gaius Patricius. Cospatrick (*c.* 1040–73), son of Malcolm (brother of 'the gracious Duncan' in Shakespeare's *Macbeth*), and Ealdgith, daughter of Uchtred, Earl of Northumbria, was probably named after his mother's half-brother. From him descended the old earls of Dunbar, several of whom bore the name, variously rendered Cospatric, Cospatrick and Gospatrick. The name has been used sparingly since the twelfth century, when that family favoured Patrick. Alexander, 10th Earl of Home, named a son Cospatrick Alexander in 1799, and he succeeded his father, He, too, named a son Cospatrick in 1848. More recently that family, and also the Dunbars of Hempriggs and the Dunbars of Durn, have used Cospatrick as a middle name.

COURTNEY, COURTENAY (m) This is the surname of an aristocratic family whose ancestors came from Courtney in France. The spelling Courteney was in favour in the nineteenth century, but Courtney as a forename is now almost universal.

CRAIG (m) This is an old surname which occurs in various localities, from *creag*, or a rocky hill. Johnannes del Craig witnessed a charter by William the Lion (1165–1214). Although all families so named did not descend from a common ancestor, there was a recognised chief in the fifteenth century, styled 'of that Ilk'. John Craig was a colleague of John Knox. Craig came to be used as a forename, and is now very popular. Creag is a variant.

CRISPIN (m) Lat. *Crispinus*, a Roman cognomen possibly derived from *crispus*, 'curled'. St Crispin was a shoemaker and therefore chosen for the patron saint of the craft. Henry V of England fought the Battle of Agincourt in 1415, on St Crispin's Day, 25 October. The variant spelling Crispian appears in a Shakespearean play, and both forms enjoyed favour for a time, but seldom appear today. Sir Crispin Agnew of Lochnaw, Baronet, is chief of the Agnews, and an advocate at the Scottish Bar.

CUTHBERT (m) O.E., a compound of *cuth*, 'famous', and *beorht*, 'bright'. St Cuthbert (died 687), Bishop of Lindisfarne, interred at Durham Cathedral, is said to have worked many miracles. There are numerous church dedications to him, including the West Kirk of Edinburgh. The name was used throughout the Middle Ages. Cuthbert the Dean is mentioned in a document relating to St Andrews about the middle of the twelfth century. Cuthbert Colville had an annual pension of £10 from the lands of Drumcross in West Lothian, between 1465 and 1474. Cuthbert Grant, 'Warden of the Plains', in Canada, was a fur-trader early in the nineteenth century, and the son of a Scots immigrant. During the First World War (1914–18), Cuthbert was used as a slang term for an evader of military service and this has contributed to its decline as a Christian name. It is however, along with Cuthbertson, an old surname.

CYBIL (f) Gr., 'prophetess', derived from Cybile of the Greeks, who originated ancient oracles propagated by the Jews and Christians. It is usually Latinised Sibella, Sibilla, Sibylla or Sibulla, but now generally rendered Sibyl or Sybil. Alexander I, who succeeded his brother Edgar as King of Scots in 1106–7, married Sibilla, a natural daughter of Henry, the English king. She died in 1122. James Primrose, WS, who died in 1641, married as his first wife Sibylla Miller, and they were ancestors of the earls of Rosebery. They also had a daughter Sibylla. Cybill Shepherd, American film actress, has made some memorable pictures. Pet forms of the name are Sib and Sibbie.

CYNTHIA (f) Gr. *Kynthia*, a title of Artemis, the 'Goddess of Cynthus', from Mount Cynthos on the isle of Delos. It was a literary name in the seventeenth century and later by various writers. Lady Cynthia, in Scott's *Peveril of the Peak*, appears as a lady of 'bewitching sorceries', who captivated the young Earl of Derby. The name has largely given way to its short form, CINDY.

CYRIL (m) Gr. *kyrillos*, 'lordly'. There were two saints of the name in the fourth century and in the fifth. A ninth-century St Cyril introduced Christianity to the Slavs and devised an alphabet. The name appears in England in the seventeenth century but made little headway until the nineteenth. It is not prolific in Scotland.

D

DALE (m) This is a surname of local origin, derived from a small glen or hollow, and may be an English form of Dair. It come into use as a forename since the nineteenth century. Johannes de Dale was a charter witness at Yester in 1374. The American writer Dale Carnegie, author of the book *How to Win Friends and Influence People*, doubtless affected use of the name in the USA. In recent years it has made headway in Scotland.

DAMIAN, DAMIEN (m) Gr., probably from *damazein*, 'to tame'. St Damianus in the fifth century was a patron of physicians. In the Middle Ages it was much in use as an ecclesiastical name. Variant forms are Damon, Daemon, Daman and Damen. Damian and Damien are currently in favour in Scotland.

DAN (m) Usually a short form of DANIEL, but was used independently at an early period. In the Bible Dan appears as one of the twelve sons of Jacob and progenitor of one of the twelve tribes. He and his brother Naphtali were sons of Bilbah, servant of RACHEL (OT, Genesis 30:5–7). In Scott's *Guy Mannering*, Dan Dunkieson is the owner of a pair of plated stirrups borrowed for 'the young Laird's use'.

DANIEL (m) Heb., 'God has judged', a biblical name (OT, Daniel 2:18). Daniel was a hero of Jewish folklore, and a number of stories were told of him. That concerning him in the lion's den gave the name popularity all over Europe. In Celtic countries such as Wales, Ireland and Scotland, the name is often synonymous with Domhnall (Donald). Short forms are Dan and Danny. The name has had something of a revival in recent years, and is in the top ten boys' names. Feminine forms are Daniella, DANIELLE and Danielc.

DANIELLE (f) French feminine form of DANIEL, and popular in Scotland today.

DAPHNE (f) Gr., 'laurel'. In classical mythology Daphne was the name of a nymph whom the god Apollo loved. She was turned into a laurel bush when she fled him. Although found on early Christian monuments, the name did not appear in Britain until the nineteenth century. It was given a boost by Daphne Du Maurier (1907–89), the novelist, but is not now fashionable.

DARREN (m) An Irish surname now popular as a forename in Scotland. It seems probable that actor Darren McGavin, born 1922, helped popularise the name. Moreover, in the TV series *Bewitched*, the leading male actor was named Darrin. Other variant spellings are Darryn and Daryn.

DARYL (m) Probably derived from d'Airel, a Normandy place-name. Darrell appears on the *Roll of Battle Abbey*, AD 1066. The name reached Scotland by the close of the thirteenth century. Gilbert Darel of Peeblesshire, swore fealty to Edward I of England in 1296. The use as a forename may not be older than the nineteenth century, but is now within the top hundred boys' names registered in Scotland.

DAVID (m) Heb., 'beloved'. Originally a lullaby word equivalent to 'darling'. In the scriptures David was the youth, armour-bearer to Saul, who slew Goliath (OT, Samuel 17:48–51). He became second king of Israel and writer of the psalms. St David, who flourished in the seventh century became the patron saint of Wales. The Celtic form was *Dathi* or *Daibhidh*. The name was much favoured in the Lower Middle Ages, and Charlemange affected it in his correspondence with Alcuin. In Scotland it was the name of two kings who reigned 1124–53 and 1329–71. The first was son of Malcolm Canmore and the saintly Queen Margaret, none of whose children were given the names of Scottish or Pictish kings. As David was the youngest child, and the Queen had no hope of more children, he was given the name of the youngest son of the biblical Jesse. David II was the son of Robert the Bruce and his second wife, Lady Elizabeth de Burgh. David is one of the most popular forenames in Scotland, and resulted in the surnames Davidson, Davison and Dawson. David Ritchie (1741–1811), the original of Scott's novel *The Black Dwarf*, was a misshapen little man who lived at Old Woodhouse near Peebles. Pet forms of the name are Dave, Davie, Davy and Davit. An old feminine pet form, Davidina, has given way to DAVINA.

DAVINA (m) Feminine form of DAVID, in current use in Scotland.

DAWN (f) The name came into use in the nineteenth century, but in its original Latin form, AURORA, meaning 'dawn'. It has been recorded in Britain since the sixteenth century. The actress Nyree Dawn Porter may have influenced use of the name. Variants are Dawna, Dawne, Dawnette and Dawnielle.

DEAN (m) A surname now popular as a Christian name. There was a place named Den in the parish of Kildrummy, Aberdeenshire, and in 1345 there was a canon of Dunkeld recorded as Robert de Den. There was also Dean in Ayrshire, an ancient home of the Boyds, Earls of Kilmarnock. It is uncertain if either influenced the use of the name Deans around Hawick in the sixteenth century. As a surname Dean probably means 'small glen'. James Dean (1931–55), American actor, who has become a cult figure, has kept the name before the public in America. The actor/singer, Dean Martin, born in 1917, may have influenced the use of the forename. It is now within the top fifty names in Scotland. The feminine form is DEANNA.

DEANNA (f) A name made famous by the singer/actress, Deanna Durban, now living in France.

DEBORAH (f) Heb., 'bee'. The biblical DEBORAH was wife of Lapidoth, and prophetess and judge of Israel who gave decisions under her palm tree on Mt Ephraim (OT, Judges 4:4–5). The screen actress, Deborah Kerr (Kerr-Trimmer), was born in Helensburgh, Dunbartonshire in 1921. Short forms are Deb, Debbie and Debby. In Ireland Deborah is sometimes used to represent *Gobnait* (ABIGAIL).

DECLAN (m) Derived from Deaglan, an Irish saint. The name has enjoyed popularity in Scotland and Ireland in recent years. Decla has been recorded as a feminine form.

DEIRDRE (f) Gael., 'sorrowful'. The name of a character in Irish and Scottish legend. Beautiful and wise, she left Ireland to marry the man of her choice and lived with him and his two brothers – sons of *Uisliu*, later *Uisneach* – near Loch Etive in Argyll. Tempted back to Ireland by a false offer of friendship, the three men were killed. Deirdre, sorrowful, took her own life. Curiously the name only became popular after the late-nineteenth-century revival of interest in matters Celtic. Fiona Macleod (William Sharp, 1856–1905), produced a novel titled *Deirdre* in 1903. The name came more into use in the 1920s. Variant spellings are Deidrie, Deidra and Dierdrie.

DENISE (f) Feminine form of DENNIS. Although outwith the top one hundred names in Scotland, it is still in regular use.

DENNIS (m) Fr., derived from the personal name Denis (earlier Denys), it is a form of the Latin *Dionysius*, the name of the Areopagite converted by St Paul of Athens (NT, Acts 17:34). It was the name of several saints including the apostle martyred near Paris in 272, who became St Denys, the patron saint of France. The name reached England towards the close of the twelfth century, and many churches there are dedicated to him. Dennys and variants have been recorded in Scotland since the late fifteenth century, and apparent in the surnames Dennis, Dennison, Denny and Dennett. The place-name Denniston, Glasgow, is a corruption of Danielston. In Ireland Denis has been used as a substitute for *Donnchadh* (DUNCAN).

DEREK (m) O.G., *Theodoric*, 'people's ruler'. It came into use in Britain in the nineteenth century and reached its peak in Scotland just before the Second World War (1939–45). The British actors Derek Bond, Derek Farr and Derek Nimmo, have probably played a part in its continuance. Dirk, a Dutch form, has doubtless been influenced by the actor Dirk Bogarde. Variant spellings of Derek are Dereck, Derrick, Derrek, Deryck and

Deryke.

DERMOT (m) Irish Gael., 'free from envy'. This is an anglicised form of Diarmit or Diarmid. The legendary character who bore this name eloped with the Queen of Tara. Caught by her husband, he was forced to hunt a wild boar, resulting in his death. Diarmit mac Cerbhaill was King of Ireland, 544–65, and his queen was Mughaina. Diarmit, surnamed *Dalta Daighre*, was at Kells in 814, in succession to Cellach, who died in 815 as Abbot of Iona. Diarmit succeeded him and was killed by the Danes, *c.* 831. The name gave rise to the prolific surname of MacDiarmid (and variants), 'son of Diarmid', but was not widely used as a forename until recent years. Darby is a short form. In Ireland Dermuit is often changed to Jeremiah, although that name has a different origin.

DESMOND (m) Irish Gael., *Deas-Munster*, 'man from South Munster'. The name was used as a surname, then as a forename in Ireland. It came late to Scotland, but although not prolific is in regular use. Des is a pet name.

DEVORGILLE (f) The name was apparently short-lived, but is of great historic interest, and variously rendered as Devorgilla, Devorguilla, Dervergoil and Dervagulda. The meaning, however, is uncertain, although the second part of the compound might indicate 'servant'. At one time it was conjectured that her name was Dornagheal, meaning 'fair hands'. If the prefix could be equated with *deur*, it might be suggested her name meant 'tearful servant [of God]'. Certainly she

fervently mourned the death in 1269 of her husband,
John Balliol, Lord of Barnard Castle, whom she married in 1233. She was the daughter and co-heiress of
Alan, Lord of Galloway, by his wife, Margaret, daughter of David Earl of Huntingdon. She is famous for her
munificence in endowing Balliol College, Oxford, in
memory of her husband. She also founded Sweetheart
Abbey (New Abbey), in Dumfriesshire where she
interred Balliol's heart and was buried there in January,
1289–90. They had seven children, and the youngest
son, John, was awarded the crown of Scotland by
Edward I in 1292.

DIANA (f) Lat., 'moon goddess', and the equivalent of
the Gr. *Artemis*. She was the feminine counterpart of
Janus, the sun god, and associated with the moon and
virginity. She was also the goddess of hunting and protector of wild animals. The statue of Diane at Ephesus
was one of the wonders of the ancient world. It may
originally have been a meteorite. In the Bible we are
told (NT, Acts 19:35) it was written that the city of
Ephesus 'is a worshipper of the great goddess Diana
and of the *image* which fell from Jupiter'. In the second century AD, it was said to be a wooden statue, but
Pliny, a contempory of Minucius, tells us it was made
of ebony. The name appears in early Christian inscriptions, but Diana as a Christian name dates only from
the Renaissance. The name, with variant spellings
Diana and Dianne, has been well favoured in Scotland.
Perhaps the character, Diana Vernon, 'the heath bell of
Cheviot', in Scott's novel *Rob Roy*, has contributed to

the popularity of the name.

DIARMID (m) *See* DERMOT.

DINAH (f) Heb., 'judged, vindicated'. A biblical name (OT, Genesis, 34:1–2), Dinah was daughter of Jacob and Leah, and was defiled by Schechem, son of Hamor, a neighbouring prince and a Hittite. Anxious to remain on good terms with Jacob, he asked for Dinah as his son's wife. Her brothers Simeon and Levi agreed on condition that the Schechemites be circumcised, and they agreed. On the third day, when still sore, they were slain by Simeon and Levi. Dina is a variant, but should not be confused with DIANA. The name was popular after the Reformation, especially among the Puritans. In Scott's novel, *St Ronan's Well*, Dinah, 'a tidy young woman', is one of the attendants at the table d'hôte in the Fox Hotel, whom Mr Winterbottom permitted to wait on no one 'till all his wants were well supplied'. Currently the name is not in fashion.

DOLINA (f) Feminine form of Donald, sometimes used in the Outer Hebrides.

DONALD (m) Said to be *Domhnall*, 'world ruler' or 'world mighty', but more likely to be a combination of two words, *domb*, house and *nuall*, 'noble' signifying 'noble house'. An apt description for a clan that ruled the Hebrides from Islay for nearly 500 years. The name was brought from Ireland to Dalriada (roughly Argyll and adjacent islands), before 503, and was a favoured name in what became Scotland. Domhnall won the Battle of Magh Rath in Ireland in 637, and succeeded to the throne. His grand-nephew, Dunchadh (Donald), was Abbot of Iona, 710–17. Domhnall *Breac* succeeded his brother Conadh as King of Scots in 629 and reigned until 642. Domhnall MacAlpin succeeded his brother Kenneth as King of the united nations of the Scots of Dalriada and the Caledonian Picts, 889 to 900. The name spread to other provinces, and Donald, son of Aedh, was elected King of the Britons of Cumbria in 908. Donald, son of Reginald, was the name-father of *Clann Domhnall*. The surname was popular in the Highlands and Western Isles for long, but sank to within the thirty names recorded in Scotland in 1864. Scott makes good use of the name in his novels, including *The Antiquary*, where Donal, Lord of the Isles, is the leader of the Gaels at the Battle of Harlaw in 1411. The name has dropped further in popularity. Pet names are Don and Donnie, and feminine forms are Dona, Donalda, Donelle, Donella and Donaldina.

DONNA (f) In Italian, *donna*, Latinised *Domna*, means 'lady', or more properly 'Lady of the House'. The name came into favour in Scotland early in the present century. The American actress, Donna Reed (Donna Mullinger, born 1921), may have influenced the use of the name. Occasionally linked with Marie, Donna is within the top hundred girls' names in Scotland.

DORA (f) Formerly a diminutive of DOROTHY, this name is now used independently. It is sometimes a short form of THEODORA. Dorinda is a seldom used poetic form of eighteenth-century origin. The pet name Dorrie is shared with names such as DOREEN and DORIS.

DOREEN (f) Gael. *Diorean*, possibly an Irish rendering

of DOROTHY, but some authorities bring it from the Celtic word for 'sullen'. Edna Lyall (Ada Ellen Bayly, 1857–1903) made *Doreen* the title of a novel (1894), and it came into use in Scotland gradually. Dorrie is a pet form.

DORIS (f) Gr., 'woman from Doris', a district in Central Greece. The name was also associated with a sea-nymph in the mythology of that country. In classical literature it was a poetic name. Moreover, it was the name of a freed woman in the time of the Roman Empire. It appears in England before 1865, and in Scotland it was established by the end of the nineteenth century. Doris is sparingly used at present.

DOROTHEA, DOROTHY (f) Gr., meaning, 'Gift of God'. It is a post-biblical name, and found in most parts of Britain from the fifteenth century. The name reached as far north as Shetland. In 1630, the testament of Dorathie Johnsdochter, wife of William Moolson in Neip, Nesting, was confirmed. By that time the pet form of Dolly had become so popular that the plaything of girls was named after it. In Scotland a doll is sometimes called a 'Dorrity'. Dolly is a short form, as are Dorrie, Dot, Dottie, Dodo and Dodie. Dorothea is the French form of the name. In Gaelic Dorothy is rendered *Diorbhall*. The name is in current, but not wide use. *See also* DORA.

DOUGAL (m) Gael. *dubh-gall*, 'dark stranger'. The appellation was probably first given to the Danes by the natives of the Hebrides. Dubh, son of Malcolm I, King of Scots, came to power in 962, but was expelled in

967. Dubhgall, son of Somerled of the Isles and his wife Raghnaid, daughter of Olaf of Man, was given the lordship of Lorne and was ancestor of the MacDugals or MacDougals. Dugal, or variant spellings such as DUGALD and Dougald, became popular forenames in the Highlands and Islands. Doug is a pet name, also applied to Douglas.

DOUGLAS (m, f) Gael. *dubh-glas*, 'dark water', from a stream in the lordship of Douglas, in Lanarkshire. William de Duglas witnessed charters between 1175 and 1200. The family figured prominently in Scottish history and was rewarded with titles and estates. Two important lines were the Red and the Black Douglases. Like other such names, Douglas was also a Christian name, found in England as well as in Scotland, and was sometimes given to girls. The actors Douglas Fairbanks, Sr (1883–1939) and Jr (1909–2000), kept the name before the public. Moreover, General Douglas MacArthur (1880–1964), the American military commander, who was of Scots descent, influenced use of the name. Pet forms are Doug, Dougie, Dug and Duggie.

DREW (m) Fr., 'sturdy', derived from the O.G. *drogo*, and introduced to Britain at the Conquest. The name also occurs in Old Welsh. In Scotland it is used as a short form of ANDREW.

DRUSILLA (f) Lat. *Drusus*, a cognomen in use in the Livian *gens*, first assumed by the Livius who killed the Gaul *Drausus*. Livia *Drusilla* was the second wife of Augustus. Drusilla, a Jewess, daughter of Agrippa I, King of Judea, a woman of great beauty, married

Antonius Felix (NT, Acts 24:24). She was lured away from her former husband Azis. The name was quite popular at one period, but is rare today. Recorded variants are Drucella, Drucilla, Druscilla and Drewsila. Cilla was sometimes a short form, but is more often a diminutive of PRISCILLA.

DUGALD (m) A variant of DOUGAL or Dugal. In Scott's novel, *A Legend of Montrose*, Dugald Dalgetty is an irrepressibly loquacious and conceited mercenary who fought under Gustavus Adolphus of Sweden, and joined the army of Montrose, well equipped for conflict. The prototype of Dugald was Robert Munro (*c*. 1600–60), who fought in the Thirty Years War. In the novelist's story, *The Antiquary*, Dugald Gunn is an old fellow soldier of Edie Ochiltree.

DUNCAN (m) Gael. *dun-chadh*, 'brown warrior'. Probably of Irish origin, it is found early as Donnachadh and Dunchadh. Duncan was Abbot of Iona, 710–17. Dunnchadh, surnamed Ua Robhacain, was coarb of Iona, 986–989. Donnchadh, lay abbot of Dunkeld, was killed in battle in 965. Two Scottish kings bore the name. Duncan, son of Crinan the Thane, was King of Scots, 1034–40, and Duncan, son of Malcolm III and Ingiborge, was king in 1094. The name occurs regularly among the noble families of Scotland as a forename and became also a surname. Duncan, Earl of Orkney, is on record in 875. One of the most famous bearers of the name was Duncan *Ban* MacIntyre (1724–1812), a gamekeeper in Rannoch, who was a Gaelic poet. Pet names are Dunc and Dunkie.

DYLAN (m) Welsh, traditionally 'son of the waves'. It was the name of a legendary sea-god, for whom the waves wept when he died. The name was made well-known by the Welsh poet, Dylan Thomas (1914–53), and is now in regular but quiet use in Scotland.

E

EACHIN, EACHUNN *See* HECTOR.

EBENEZER (m) Heb., 'stone of help', derived from a stone raised by Samuel to mark the defeat of the Philistines and called Ebenezer (OT, Samuel 7:12). The name became popular in Scotland after the Reformation and was borne by a number of notable people. The Rev. Ebenezer Erskine (1680–1754) founded the Secession Church. Ebenezer Michie (1766–1812), schoolmaster at Cleish, Kinross-shire, had a mock epitaph written by Robert Burns. Ebenezer Forsyth (1816–73), editor and proprietor of the *Inverness Advertiser*, was a keen Shakespearean. In Scott's *Waverley*, Ebenezer Cruickshanks is landlord of the 'seven branched Golden Candlestick'. Charles Dickens's character 'Ebenezer Scrooge' did not immediately affect the popularity of the name, but it is now in decline. Variant spellings are Ebbaneza, Ebeneezer and Ebenezar. Abe is a short form and Abie a pet name.

EDGAR (m) OE. *ead-gar*, 'happy spear'. Eadgar, a younger son of Malcolm III (1057–93) wore the crown from 1097–1107, although in England for part of that period. In England, King Edgar, grandson of King Alfred, reigned 944–75, and, being a peaceable man, gave the name popularity. The name was used as a surname, especially in Nithsdale, but the bearers were of Celtic origin. As a Christian name Edgar has been used sporadically, but it was revived by writers of fiction in the nineteenth century. In *The Fair Maid of Perth*, Scott makes Edgar purse-bearer to the Duke of Rothesay, and in his novel *The Bride of Lammermoor*, his hero is Edgar, Master of Ravenswood.

EDITH (f) O.E. *ead*, 'rich', and *gyo*, 'war'. Eadgyth was the name of two early saints. Edgitha, daughter of Godwin, Earl of Wessex, married the Saxon king Edward the Confessor (1004–66). Edith, variously called MAUD or MATILDA, daughter of Malcolm II, King of Scots, married King Henry of England in 1100. The name remained popular throughout the Middle Ages, but went out of favour after the Reformation, only to make a revival in the nineteenth century. Among famous bearers of the name were Nurse Edith Cavell (1865–1915), Dame Edith Sitwell (died 1964), and the actress Dame Edith Evans (died 1976). In Scott's *Ivanhoe*, Edith, 'of a dignified mein', is the widow of Atheling. Edith, granddaughter of Lady Margaret, liferentrix of Tullietudlem, appears in his novel *Old Mortality*. In his poem 'The Lord of the Isles', Edith is the Maid of Lorn. Edie is a short form of the name.

EDMOND, EDMUND (m) O.E. *aed*, 'rich', and *mund*, 'protection', giving us 'rich protector'. The name of a ninth-century saint, King of the East Angles, killed by the Danes in 870, and another saint, Edmund, Archbishop of Canterbury, who died in 1240. Edmund Ironside, died 1016, the English king, fought the Danes during the reign of his father, Ethelred II. The name Laurence *filius* Aedmundi appears as witness to a charter of the lands of Gorgie (Edinburgh), c. 1200. Edmund of Fala, a younger son of Sir William Hay of Lockerworth, had a charter of Yester, Duncan Law and Morham, 1436–37. Edmond is a variant spelling, and from a person of this name Edmondstone, near Musselburgh, derived its name, which resulted in the surname, carried as far as the Shetland Isles. In Ireland Edmund was sometimes interchangeable with Edward, but in modern times Eamon is used there for the latter. Short forms are Ed and Eddie, used also for EDWARD and EDWIN.

EDWARD (m) O.E., *ead*, 'rich', and *weard*, 'guardian', usually understood as 'happy ward'. Scots will always recall Edward Longshanks, the English king who sought, by fair means and foul, to subjugate the Scots. In spite of that the name has been widely used in Scotland, both as a forename and as a surname. Edward Brus, brother of King Robert I, was crowned King of Ireland in 1316, but was killed at Dundalk in 1318. The seal of George Edward, 1441, is extant. Wattie Edward was a tenant of the 'burcht of Kethik', 1504. The name was early confused with Udard, and the old name of the family of Edward of Balruddery, in Angus, was in fact Udard. The English genealogist and author, Gerald Hamilton-Edwards (1907–87), matriculated arms in Lyon Court, Edinburgh, in 1944, as a descendant of the family of Hamilton of Muirhouse and Bardannoch. The naming of the Queen's youngest child as Edward has probably added to the popularity of the name, and it is now within the top one hundred boys' names. Short forms are Ned and Neddie, Ted and Teddie, but Ed and Eddie are more highly favoured. The Gaelic form is *Eideard*.

EDWIN (m) O.E. *Ead-wine*, 'happy friend'. Edwyn was the name of a Northumbrian king who married Ethelburga, a Kentish princess, and died in 633. Folk-etymology has connected the name with Edinburgh, but it is extremely unlikely that this king had any connection with Edinburgh. It bore the pre-Celtic name *Edyn* long before Edwin of Northumbria was born, and may have derived from a district such as the Braid Hills, rendered of old *Eideyn Braghaid* in Gaelic. It must be owned however, that the meaning is obscure. The name Edwin survived the Norman Conquest, and is sometimes found as a surname. It became more common in the eighteenth century, and Dickens used the name for his last novel, *Edwin Drood*. It is in current, but not wide use in Scotland today. Pet names are Ed and Eddie, The feminine form is EDWINA.

EDWINA Feminine form of EDWIN, earlier found as Edwyna.

EGIDIA (f) *See* GILES and Julia. A common name in the later Middle Ages. Egidia, daughter of Robert II, by all accounts a great beauty, married *c.* 1387, Sir William Douglas of Nithsdale. A daughter, Egidia, married *c.* 1407, Henry St Clair, Earl of Orkney. The name was in use as late as 1843, when Archibald William [Montgomerie], 13th Earl of Eglinton, had a daughter so named. However, the name had been rendered as Giles before that time. Egidia, called Giles, daughter and heiress of John Hay of Tullybody, married Alexander Seton, Lord Gordon, before 1427. Thomas Weir of Blackwood married Egidia or Giles, daughter of John, 3rd Lord Somerville, before 12 October 1483. In Scotland Giles often became JULIA.

EILIDH *See* AILEEN.

EILEEN *See* AILEEN. *My Sister Eileen*, originally a book by Ruth McKenney, later a play and a film, probably helped to spread the name.

EITHNE (f) Gael. *aodhnait*, 'little fire'. The Irish mother of St Columba (521–597) of Iona was Eithne, wife of Fedhlimidh, and she was of Leinster extraction, descended from a provincial king. It was much used as a feminine form of AIDAN. Variants on record are ETHNE, Ethna, Eithnie, Ethnea and Aithne.

ELAINE *See* AILEEN.

ELEANOR (f) A form of HELEN, introduced into England by Eleanor of Aquitane (1122–1204), who married Henry II. King Edward I married Eleanor of Castile, who died in 1290. Eleanor, daughter of James I and Joan Beaufort, married in 1449, Sigismund Von Tirol, Duke of Austria, brother of the Emperor Maximilian I.

The name has enjoyed good standing down through the ages, but in Scotland is now outwith the top one hundred girls' names. The form Elinor was used by Nell Gwyn (1650–87), mistress of Charles II. In modern times Eleanor Roosevelt (1884–1962), wife of President Franklin D Roosevelt, gave the name prominence in America. LEONORA is possibly derived from Eleanor. Pet forms are Ella, NORA, Nell and Nellie.

ELI (m) Heb., 'height'. The biblical Eli was a prophet of Shiloh and exemplar of the venerable man whose offspring are disappointing. He looked after SAMUEL in the temple. The name became common in the seventeenth and eighteenth centuries, but is now rare. It is occasionally found as Ely. The talented actor, Eli Wallach, born 1915, has given the name prominence in America. It is sometimes a short form of ELIAS.

ELIAS (m) Heb. A short form of the biblical Elijah, 'Jehovah is my God'. Elijah was the Tishbite prophet of the ninth century, who championed the Jewish religion against Ahab, who introduced the cult of Baal into Israel, along with his wife Jezebel (OT, 1 Kings 18:17–18). The name seems synonymous with Helias. A silversmith of this name was one of the Christians in Rome in AD 406. Helias, son of Huchtred, had a grant of the lands of Dundas, near Queensferry, by Waldeve, son of COSPATRIC, before 1145. Helya, a canon of Glasgow, is recorded 1177–99. Elias Henderson is a chaplain in Scott's novel, *The Abbot*. The surnames Elies and Ellis derive from Elias.

ELISABETH, ELIZABETH (f) Heb., *Elisheba*, 'oath of God'.

The name evolved from the Greek *Elizabet*, through the Latin *Elizabetha*. Elizabeth was the wife of Zacharius and mother of John the Baptist (NT, Luke 1:5–41). In medieval times Elizabeth was often rendered ISOBEL. The spelling Elisabeth is continental but appears frequently in Scotland. St Elisabeth of Hungary, who died *c*. 1210, probably influenced the use of the name. Elizabeth Douglas, Maid of Honour to Joanna, Queen of James I, is famous as the heroine who attempted to prevent the assassination of the king at Perth, 1436–37, by thrusting her arm into the staples of a door. She has come down to us erroneously as 'Kate-barlass'. The poet Burns had two natural daughters named Elizabeth, namely Elizabeth Paton (1784–1817) and Elizabeth Park (1791–1873). His legitimate daughter Elizabeth, named after Mrs Riddell, died young in 1795. Elizabeth, Queen of England, appears in Scott's novel, *Kenilworth*. *Elisaid* or *Elasaid* is the Gaelic form. Elasaid nic Nuier (1787–1871) is buried at Kilmodan, in a MacIlleain lair. The Gaels also favour *Beitidh*. BETHIA is sometimes used as a variant spelling, but has a different origin. Elizabeth has more variants than any other female name. These include (with pet names) Bess, Bessie, Bet, Beth, Bette, Betty, Bettina, Betsy, Eli, Elizabetta, Eliza, Elise, Elsie, Elsa, Illse, Lalla, Lib, Libby, Lisa, Liz, Liza, Lizzie, Leezie, Lisbeth, Lisabeth, Lizabeth, Lisette, Leise, Tetty and Tetsy.

ELLA (f) O.G., 'all'. Came to Britain as a Norman-French name, variants of which are Ala and Ela, common in the post-Conquest era. The name was revived in the

nineteenth century and is often found as a pet name for
ELLEN or HELEN.

ELLEN (f) An older English form of HELEN, now used
independently and popular in Scotland. It is cognate
with Elena, found as early as the fourteenth century.
Ella and Nell are sometimes found as pet names.

ELIOT, ELLIOTT (m) A well-known Border surname,
derived from the O.E. *Aelfwald*, often rendered Elwald
or Elwold, both of which forms became obsolete, but
survived as surnames. Eliot and Elliott as surnames
have many variants, but both appear now also as forenames.

ELSIE (f) Elsie and Elsa can be independent names, but
there is much confusion as both appear occasionally as short forms of ELSPETH (itself often a variant
of ELIZABETH) and ALISON. It can also come from
ISABEL. The Highland historian and folklorist, Dr
Isabel Frances Grant (1887–1983), was known to
friends such as Dame Flora MacLeod of MacLeod as
Elsie. In Longfellow's *The Golden Legend*, Elsie is the
daughter of Gottlieb, a farm tenant of Prince Henry
of Hoheneck, who was willing to give up her life to
cure the Prince of some malady. The name should not
be confused with Ailsa, a forename derived from the
island rock of Ailsa Craig.

ELSPETH (f) In Scotland Elspeth is often a variant of
ELIZABETH, and is sometimes curtailed to Elspet, Eppy
or Elspat. The name is found in Scott's *Guy Mannering*
as 'the bedral's widow', to whom Dandy Dinmont suggested the new cottage at Derncleugh should be given.

In his *Rob Roy*, Elspeth MacFarlane is Bailie Nicol Jarvie's mother.

EMANUEL (m) Heb., 'God is with us'. The biblical Emanuel (OT, Isaiah 7:14) was the name given for the promised child of a virgin. The name was not much used in the Middle Ages, but became more frequent in the seventeenth century. Anthony Haig of Bemersyde had a son Emmanuel, 1666–99. In modern times one of the best-known persons of that name was Emmanuel Shinwell (1884–1986), MP for Linlithgow, 1922–24, and 1928–31. Manuel is a short form used mainly in the USA. Mannie is a pet name, and feminine forms are Emanuela and Manuela.

EMELINE (f) Of Teutonic origin, this name, rendered so in French, and possibly meaning 'labour', should not be confused with EMILIA or EMILY, but may be cognate with EMMA. Variants include Emaline, Emiline, Emelen, Emylin, Emmalene and Emblyn.

EMILIA (f) A feminine form of AEMILIUS. For a long period the name was quite common but now appears as EMILY. Emilia Murray, daughter of John, Marquess of Atholl, married Hugh Fraser, Lord Lovat in 1685. They had a daughter Anne, who married Norman MacLeod of MacLeod, and they, too, had a daughter Emilia. Later, John MacLeod of MacLeod married Emilia, daughter of Alexander Brodie of that Ilk, Lord Lyon, and died in 1767. Percy Shelley's poem, 'Epipsychidion' is addressed to Emilia Viviani, a lady in whom he thought he had found a visionary soul in harmony with his own. Amelia is another form. King George III's daughter, Princess

Amelia, was usually called Emily. Emmeliné derives from the old French diminutives of Emilia and Emily.

EMILY (f) Popular equivalent of EMILIA. James 3rd Duke of Montrose had a daughter Emily (1805–1900), who was widow of Edward T. Foley for fifty-three years. Emmie and Milly are diminutives.

EMMA (f) O.G., *irmin*, 'universal'. The name was brought to Britain by Emma, daughter of Richard I, Duke of Normandy, and she married (1) 1002, Ethelred the Unready; (2) 1007, King Cnut. It was a favourite Norman name which became more common after 1066. In the Middle Ages it led to surnames such as Emmet and Emmot. In Scotland, Philip de Seton, who flourished in the late twelfth century, had a daughter Emma, who married Adam de Pollisworth. The mistress of Lord Nelson was Lady Emma Hamilton (1761–1815). Emma has had an astonishing rise to prominence and is now one of the most prolific girls' names in Scotland. It appears often in combinations such as Emma-Jane, Emma Jayne and Emma Louise.

ENOCH (m) Heb., meaning 'skilled'. The first biblical Enoch was the son of Cain, eldest son of ADAM and EVE (OT, Genesis 4:17). Another, father of Methuselah, 'walked with God', without it seems, suffering death (Genesis 5:24). The name was favoured by the Puritans, but reached its highest popularity after the publication in 1864 of Tennyson's poem, 'Enoch Arden'. The best known Briton bearing the name was the veteran scholar and politician, Enoch Powell. The name is rare in Scotland.

EOGHAN *See* EUGENE.

EPHRAIM (m) Gr., 'fruitful'. Ephraim appears in the scriptures as the second, but most favoured son of Joseph and
Asenath. Joseph's father, Jacob, favoured Ephraim, and
this was interpreted by medieval Christians as signifying the superiority of Christianity over the older Judaic
religion (OT, Genesis 41:52, 48:9-20). The name
came into use in Scotland after the Reformation, and
was used in Covenanting times. Scott makes Ephraim
MacBriar a youthful Covenanting preacher in *Old
Mortality*, and in *Rob Roy* has Mr Ephraim MacVittie,
a man 'of starched and severe aspect', as a partner in a
Glasgow firm. Robert Louis Stevenson makes Ephraim
Mackellar, an old servant, tell the story of *The Master
of Ballantrae*.

ERASMUS (m) Gr., 'desired'. The name of a fourth-century
saint, but best remembered from the Dutch scholar,
Desiderius Erasmus (Gerrit Gerritszoon, 1466–1536).
Erasmus Darwin (1731–1802), naturalist, was the
grand-father of Charles Darwin. Although used sparingly in Scotland, the name reached the Shetland Isles
early in the seventeenth century. Andrew Erasmus in
Middail, and Erasmus Johnson in Unst, died testate in
1628. The testament of Margaret Erasmusdochter was
confirmed in 1630.

ERIC (m) O.Nor., meaning 'ever brave'. The name was
brought to Britain probably by the Danes in the ninth
century, and since then has been in regular use. Eric
Slagbrellis, who ruled Orkney and Caithness with his
cousin PAUL, married a daughter of Kali (or Rognvald)

before 1170. Eric, King of Norway, married Princess Margaret of Scotland in 1281, and they were the parents of The Maid of Norway whose death in 1290 caused the great competition for the crown of Scotland. The surname Erikson is derived from Eric or Erik. Laurence Erikson in Breik, in Delting, Shetland is on record in 1633. Angus Bresone, servant, was owed his fee by William Irving, *alias* Brabner, in How, who died in 1608. Eric [MacKay] (1773–1847), 7th Lord Reay, died unmarried, leaving a natural daughter, Erica, who married in 1835, Sir Walter Minto Townsend Farquhar, Baronet. Erica was thus the feminine form of Eric. The novelist and historian, Eric Linklater (1899–1974), was of Orcadian extraction. Another notable bearer of the name was Eric Henry Liddell (1902–45), the athlete commemorated in the film *Chariots of Fire*. Rex, Rick and Rickie, shared with RICHARD, are occasionally found as pet names.

ERICA *See* ERIC.

ERIN (f) Gael. *Eireann*, 'western isle'. It is a poetic name for Ireland and has become more popular in Scotland than in the Emerald Isle. It figures in a number of songs, such as 'Come back to Erin, Mavourneen' and 'Let Erin Remember'.

ESME (m,f) Fr. 'beloved' or 'esteemed'. A male name introduced to Scotland from France by a cousin of James VI, it came into use later as a feminine name, and it may be synonymous with the French Aime (*see* AMY).

ESTHER (f) In the scriptures (OT, Esther), *Esther* is given as the Persian equivalent of the Hebrew *Hadassah*, 'myrtle', but has been said to be Persian, meaning 'star'. The myrtle was the emblem of love and sacred to Venus. Esther (interchangeable with HESTER) became one of the most celebrated heroines of antiquity. When the Palazzo Vecchio in Florence was altered to become the home of Duke Cosimo I of Tuscany, a suite was made for the Duchess and decorated with the exploits of famous women including Esther. In 1567, Walter Scott of Harden, ancestor of Sir Walter Scott, married Marion Scott, 'the flower of Yarrow', and they had a daughter Esther, who married first, Elliot of Falnash, and secondly, George Langlands of that Ilk. Pet forms of the name are Ettie, Etty, Hettie and Hetty.

ETHAN (m) Heb., 'constant'. The name is biblical (OT, 1 Kings 4:31) and is mentioned in the title of the 89th Psalm. Ethan Allan was a prominent figure before the American Revolution, but the recent rise of the name to popularity is due to the character played by the American actor, John Wayne, in the classic western film *The Searchers*. Wayne considered it his finest role and named a son Ethan.

ETHNE *See* EITHNE

EUGÉNE (m) Gael. *Aodh*, 'well born'. Uigene, 'a stingy man', was despised by St Columba. He was rich, but the saint prophesied he would become poor, and he did. St Columba had a cousin called Aedh. Aedh *Dubh*, son of Suibhne, an Irish chief, became King of Uladh, and died in 588. Eugene was the name of four popes (as Eugenius), consecrated ad, 654, 824, 1145 and 1431.

A Pictish priest living in Leinster appears as logenan. Eocha is a variant, and an Irish prince of this name was descended from Niall of the Nine Hostages. He died in 627. Owen, the Welsh form of the name, is popular in Scotland today, and Eoghan is in current use. Gene is a short form. Ewan or Euan is a common Gaelic name associated with Eugene. The feminine form is EUGENIA.

EUGÉNIA, EUGÉNIE (f) Feminine forms of EUGÉNE. The short form Ena is shared with the Irish *Aithne*, sometimes transliterated ANNA or HANNAH. The Empress Eugenie (1826–1920) was descended from the Kirkpatricks of Dumfries-shire. Her grandfather, William Kirkpatrick (1764–1837), of the Conheath family, was American consul at Malaga, Spain, and married Dona Francisca Maria, daughter of Baron de Grevignée. Their younger daughter, Eugenie Marie de Guzman, married Charles Louis Napolean III, Emperor of France, in 1853. Eugénie, daughter of the Duke and Duchess of York, is a modern instance of the name.

EUPHAME, EUPHEMIA (f) Gr., 'fair speech'. The name appears on early Christian monuments, and St Euphemia was a fourth-century martyr whose cult was widespread in the east. It occurs from the twelfth century as Eufemia and Euphame. The name, in various spellings, became more common in Scotland than elsewhere. Euphemia, daughter of Ferquhard, Earl of Ross, who died *c.* 1251, married Walter de Moravia, Lord of Duffus. Euphame McCalzean, daughter of Lord Cliftonhall, a Senator of the College of Justice, was a notorious witch who was sentenced to be burned alive on the Castle Hill of Edinburgh in 1591. In the parochial registers of Dalgetty, Fife, 'Youfimey', daughter of Alexander and Margaret Henderson in Fordell was registered in 1789. Variants are Eupham, Eufan and Euphan, and short forms are Eppie, Effie, Phemie and occasionally Fanny. The Gaelic form is *Oighrig*.

EUSTACE (m) Gr., 'fruitful'. Because of two saints named Eustacius, the name was in use in Britain before the Norman Conquest of 1066, and it remained popular during the rest of the Middle Ages. Sir Eustace Maxwell of Caerlaverock held that castle for the English king in 1312. He changed sides twice during the War of Independence. Eustas and Eustis are variant spellings. The surnames Stacey and Stacey derive from short forms of Eustace, which itself came also to be used as a surname. The feminine form is EUSTACIA. See also ANASTASIA.

EUSTACIA (f) Feminine form of EUSTACE. Eustacia, daughter of William Colville, who died *c.* 1280, ancestor of the Lords Colville of Culross, married (as his second wife) Reginald le Cheyne, and was widowed by 1296, when she rendered homage to King Edward I.

EVA *See* EVE.

EVALINE (f) O.G. *Avelinea*, 'hazel nut', through the French form Aveline. The name came to Britain with the Normans, and gave rise to surnames such as Evelyn and Eveling. Evelyn is a common variant and has been used as a masculine name. It is often used to transliterate the Gaelic *Eighilin*, meaning 'light'. Evelyn, Baroness

Gray, born 1841, married in 1863, James M. Smith, who assumed the name and arms of Gray, in addition to Smith. Evelyn Beringer, Sir Raymond's daughter, is the heroine in Scott's novel, *The Betrothed*.

EVAN (m) Welsh form of JOHN, but occasionally confused in Scotland with Euan or EWAN. Evan *Dhu* of Lochiel, in Scott's *Legend of Montrose*, is one of the Highland chiefs who placed themselves under Montrose at Darnlinvarach. The name is in current, but quiet use.

EVANDER (m) Gr., 'good man'. In classical mythology, Evander or Euander, son of Hermes and Carmenta, led a colony from Passantuem in Arcadia into Latium, and built a city on the Palatine Hill, sixty years after the Trojan War. Evander Murchieson of Octertier took the hated 'Test' in Ross-shire in 1685. Edward MacIver (1787–1861) emigrated from the island of Pabbay, off Lewis, to Richmond County, Quebec, Canada, in 1841, with his family, including a son Evander (1827–92). Evander became a Lowland form of IVAR and MacIvar. The Gaelic form is *Iomhar*.

EVE, (f) Heb. *havvah*, 'life-giving'. The first woman, according to the Bible (OT, Genesis 3:20), who had three sons by ADAM; Cain, Abel and Seth. Adam and Eve lost their innocence in the Garden of Eden, thus committing original sin. The name was well used in the Middle Ages. Eva, a variant spelling, heiress of Garnait, was the wife of Colbain, Mormaer of Buchan, *c*. 1140. Eva, another heiress, daughter of Dougal *Doul*, 6th chief of Clan Chattan, married in 1291, Angus Mackintosh of Mackintosh, who became 7th chief of Clan Chattan. Both Eva and Eve are in current use in Scotland, but neither is prolific. In Ireland it was substituted for the earlier Gaelic *Aoiffe*, meaning 'pleasant'.

EVELYN *See* EVALINE.

EWAN, EUAN (m) Gael., from *eobhann* or *eoghan*, 'youth'. Both spellings appear, and also Ewir. It is sometimes associated with EUGENE. The name has always been popular in Gaeldom. There was a small Clan Ewen. The Rev. Alexander Macfarlane, in his account of the Parish of Kilfinan (*Old Statistical Account*) notes the remains of a building called *Caisteal Mhic Eobhuin*, i.e. 'MacEwan's Castle', on the shores of Loch Fyne. This MacEwan was the chief of the clan and owner of part of Kilfinan parish, but the property passed to the Campbells. Ewan is still much used as both forename and surname. EUGÉNE is sometimes used for Ewan or Euan.

EZRA (m) Heb., 'help'. Ezra or Esdras, a priestly scholar, was one of the architects of the survival of the religion and identity of the Jewish race. His name is attached to two books in the *Apocrypha*. The Puritans adopted Ezra as a forename in the seventeenth century, but the name was never prolific. R.W. Mackenna, in his sketch of 'James Burnie, Shoemaker', in *Bracken and Thistledown*, has Ezra Snubb as the Dalbean wright and undertaker. In modern times the most distinguished person to bear the name was Ezra Pound (1885–1972), the American poet and composer.

F

FANNY *See* EUPHEMIA and FRANCES

FARQUHAR (m) Gael. *fear-char*, 'friendly one', or 'very dear one'. It is variously written Fearchar, Feachar and Fearchair, but corrupt spellings occur in medieval records. Fearchar *Fada*, ruler of the Scottish kingdom of Dalriada, died in 697. Farchard, *judex de* Buchan, witnessed a charter by the Earl of Buchan, *c.* 1200. Fercardus *seneschallus de* Badenoch is on record in 1234. The name appears also as a surname. Schir Matthew Farquhar, cleric in Kirkwall, appears in 1520. Farquhar was a favoured forename among the Highland clans. Farquhar Campbell from Argyll emigrated to Cumberland County, North Caroline, before 1764, and became a member of the senate. Farquharson 'son of Farquhar', is a clan name, and those of Aberdeenshire descend from a grandson of the Laird of Mackintosh who arrived in the county before 1382. Ferquhard was much favoured by the Cumings of Badenoch in the fourteenth century.

FELICIA (f) Feminine form of FELIX, and in Scotland found more often in the variant spelling, Felicity. The name appears on early Christian monuments, and forms such as Phelicia and Philicia are on record. Pet names are Luckie and Lucky.

FELIX (m) Lat. *felix*, 'happy'. The name of several saints and five popes, consecrated 269, 356 (anti-pope), 483,

526 and 1439. The biblical Felix was Antonius, governor or procurator of Judaea, AD 52–60, who married Drusilla, daughter of Herod Agrippa I. His term of office saw much crime, disorder and corruption (NT, Acts 23:26–35). Felix, Bishop of Moray, is on record in 1165. The name came more into use in the nineteenth century but has never been prolific. Felix Hudson (1923–93), a Dunfermline antique dealer, was a noted horologist. The feminine form is FELICIA.

FENELLA (f) Gael. *Fionnaghal*, from *fionn*, 'white', and *guala*, 'shoulder'. Finguala or Fynvola, daughter of Torquil MacLeod, IVth of Lewis, married before 1346, Kenneth MacKenzie of Kintail, ancestor of the Earls of Seaforth. Fingoll Neine-Ane, wife of John Barron Fraser, probably of the family of Macpherson of Brin, is on record in 1577. Scott popularised the name Fenella in *Peveril of the Peak*. Occasionally it has been associated with FLORA.

FERGUS (m) Gael. *Fear-ghur*, 'super choice'. Fergus mac Erc led colonists from Ireland into Dalriada (roughly Argyll and the adjacent islands) about AD 503. Fergna the Briton, otherwise Fergus Brit, was second Abbot of Iona, 605–623, and Fergus the Pict was a bishop in Ireland in 721. Pictish names have come down to us as Urguist, Wirguist and Wrguist. One of the small tribes in Dalriada was the *Cinel Fergus Salach*. In the south-west there was a race descended from Fergus, Lord of Galloway, whose followers fought at the Battle of the Standard in 1138. MacFergus or Ferguson, 'son of Fergus', evolved as a surname, and there was a

Perthshire clan of this name attached to the Murrays. The Fergusons of Kilkerran, in Ayrshire, seem to be of different origin. Fergie is a short form, and the feminine form is FERGUSIA.

FERGUSIA (f) Feminine form of FERGUS, not now fashionable. Fergusia, elder daughter of Sir George Wishart of Cliftonhall, Baronet, married George Lockhart (1700–61) of Carnwath. The name honoured her maternal grandfather, Fergus McCubbin, of Knockdolian, in Ayrshire.

FINAN (m) Gael., but the meaning is obscure. The earliest-known person of the name was a Scot from Iona, who was Bishop of Lindisfarne, *c*. 651–61. The MacLennans derive their patronymic from MacGill'inan, whose father, *Gillie Fhinan*, in the thirteenth century, was named in honour of the Irish Saint Finan. Finan also became a personal name in the Highlands. In 1785, Finan MacDonald (1782–1851) of Loch Hourne, Knoydart, emigrated to Canada with his parents. As a member of the North-West Company of Montreal, he explored the basins of the Columbia, Kootenai and Snake Rivers with David Thompson (1770–1857), the geographer.

FINLAY (m) Gael. *Fionnladh*, 'fair hero'. In the Gaelic MS of 1467 (Advocates Ms 72.1.1. National Library of Scotland), the name occurs in the genitive as *Finlaec*, and in the *Duan Albanach*, an old poetic chronicle of the kings of Dalriada, *c*. 1070, as *Fionnlaoich*. In various sources the name of MacBeth's father is given as *Findlaech* and *Finnleikr* (Gaelic and Norse), who died *c.* 1020. The name is not uncommon in early Scottish records, and has continued in regular use, although outwith the top one hundred boys' names. It gave rise to the surname Finlayson 'son of Finlay'. Findla *Mor*, ancestor of the Farquharsons of Invercauld, a man of courage and daring, was killed at Pinkie in 1547. Finlay MacKenzie, a cooper of Stornoway, emigrated to Philadelphia on the ship *Friendship* in 1774.

FIONA (f) Gael. 'fair' or 'white'. It has been said that the name is no older than the time of James 'Ossian' Macpherson (1736–96), but Fione and her husband, Reginald, Lord of the Isles, gave an endowment to Paisley Abbey, *c.* 1175. It is possibly a feminine form of Fion or Fingal. A legendary Gaelic giant, Fion mac Comnal, could place his feet on two mountains and stoop to drink from a stream in the glen below. Fiona MacLeod was the pen-name of William Sharp (1856–1905), a Paisley-born miscellaneous writer in prose and verse. In the big screen musical, *Brigadoon*, Cyd Charisse played the part of Fiona Campbell. Ffyona Campbell completed a round-the-world walk in October, 1994. Fhiona is another variant spelling.

FLORA (f) Lat. *flos*, 'flower', the name given to the Roman goddess of flowers. It appeared in France as a forename at the Renaissance, from where it was carried to Scotland. Occasionally it has been used as an alternative to FENELLA. Flora Macdonald (1722–90), the Jacobite heroine of 1745, increased the popularity of the name. Short forms are Florrie and Flory, and pet names are Flo and Flossy.

FLORENCE (m,f) Lat. *Florentius*, 'flourishing'. On early
   Christian monuments the name appears for males and
   females and this practice continued in Scotland rather
   longer than it did in England. The name Florentius
   appears on an ancient monument at Whithorn.
   Florence, son of Florence III, Count of Holland, and
   Ada, granddaughter of King David I, was Bishop-
   elect of Glasgow in 1202. Florence Wilson of Moray,
   was one of the foremost Latin scholars of Europe in
   the sixteenth century. The name came to be used as
   a Christian name for girls. Florence, daughter of
   Tormod MacLeod of that Ilk, who died in 1585, married Lachlan MacLean of Coll. Later MacLeod women
   bore the name. In more recent times, the Crimean War
   nurse, Florence Nightingale – born in the Italian city of
   the name – shed lustre on the name. The name shares
   the short forms and pet names applied to FLORA.

FRANCES (f) The feminine form of FRANCIS has been
   in use since the seventeenth century. It is rendered
   Fràngag in Gaelic. Frances Teresa, daughter of Dr
   Walter Stewart, son of the first Lord Blantyre, was
   loved by Charles II, and in 1666–7 married Charles,
   Duke of Richmond. She served as a model for the figure of Britannia, long used on the copper coinage of
   Britain. Mrs Frances Ann Dunlop, née Wallace (1730–
   1815), was a friend of the poet Burns, who named one
   of his sons after her, and Francis Grose (1731–91),
   the English antiquary, who visited the bard when he
   lived at The Isle, before moving into his Dumfriesshire
   farm. Short forms and pet names are Frannie, Franny,

Fanny, Francie, Frankie and Fran, some of which are now used independently.

FRANCESCA (f) The Italian form FRANCESCA is currently more popular in Scotland than FRANCES.

FRANCIS (m) Lat. *Franciscus*, 'a Frenchman'. It became a much favoured name in Europe, doubtless because of the fame of St Francis (Francesco) of Assisi (1182–1226), whose baptismal name was Giovanni. Francis was the name of German emperors and French monarchs. Francis II of France was the first husband of Mary, Queen of Scots, and this link made the name popular in Scotland. Sir Walter Scott made much use of the name, especially in his poorest novel, *Rob Roy*, in which the fictitious Osbaldistones feature more prominently than the Highlander. Father Francis appears in his *Quentin Durward* as a Franciscan friar, and another is a priest in *The Talisman*. The abbreviated form Francie is given to a 'craigsman' in *The Antiquary*. The short form Frank is often used independently. *Fraing* is the Gaelic rendering, and Frances is the feminine form.

FRASER (m) This surname has been much used in the present century as a forename, and is now within the top forty boys' names registered annually. The name was originally *de Frisselle*, *Freseliere*, or *Frisel*, derived from the French for strawberry. The latter has become an independent surname. Simon Fraser held lands in East Lothian *c.* 1180, and was probably descended from seigneurs of Freseliers in Anjou. The Frasers gained a foothold in the north and became a powerful clan. Simon C. Fraser (1911–95), Baron of Lovat, was an outstanding commando leader in the Second World War. To the Gaels he was *Mac Shimidh*, 'son of Simon'. Frazer is a variant and also now used as a Christian name.

FREDERIC, FREDERICK (m) O.G. *frid-ric*, 'peace ruler'. It was the name of several German and Prussian kings. The industrious Scottish author, Thomas Carlyle (1795–1881) compiled his largest work, *The History of Frederick the Great* of Prussia in the 1850s. The name was seldom found in Britain until favoured by the royal family. The short forms, Fred, Freddie and Freddy have all been used independently. See also FREDERICA.

FREDERICA (f) Feminine form of Frederick. It appears also as Freda, Fredalena, Fredaline, Fredith, Fredora and Fredrika. The old form, Frederickina is obsolete, and Frederica itself has one out of fashion.

G

GABRIEL (m) Heb. meaning 'man of God'. Gabriel is mentioned in the scriptures as the person whom Daniel consulted about a dream (OT, Daniel 8:16–27). In the NT, Gabriel is the Archangel of the Annunciation (Luke 1:26–35). The name has been used infrequently in Scotland since the Middle Ages, but is still in use. Gabriel Semple of Cathcart had a daughter Margaret, who married John Pollock of Pollock, who died in 1564. Gabriel Richardson (1759–1820), a brewer and a Provost of Dumfries, came into contact with Robert Burns, when the latter was an excise man, and the bard wrote a mock epitaph on him. In Scott's *Old Mortality* Gabriel Kettledrummle was an uncompromising Covenanter. The usual feminine form is GABRIELLE.

GABRIELLE (f) The French feminine form of GABRIEL is in regular use in Scotland, and also the Italian rendering, Gabriella. Lady Gabriella Marina Alexandra Ophelia, born 1981, is daughter of Prince Michael of Kent. Gabrielle Drake is a popular actress who may have influenced the use of the name. Pet forms are Gabi and Gaby.

GAIL, GAYLE (f) Pet forms of ABIGAIL which have become popular since the Second World War. The variant Gael is sometimes used, possibly to give the name a more Scottish flavour.

GARY (m) This name probably derives from Garret, a variant of GERARD, but its adoption in this country is almost entirely due to the late Holywood great star, Gary Cooper, whose film career commenced in 1927. He was born Frank Cooper, but the name was changed at the suggestion of an agent whose home town was Gary in Indiana. It ranks about twentieth in the most favoured names for boys in Scotland. Garry is a variant, but not so fashionable.

GAVIN (m) The Scottish form of the Welsh *Gawain*, 'hawk of May'. Sir Gawain became one of the best-loved characters in Arthurian legend. It is notable that in the old British kingdom of Strathclyde Gavin was both a forename and surname. As a Christian name it was much used by the Hamiltons. Gavin Hamilton, a son of James of Cadzow, who died *c.* 1439, was the Provost of the Collegiate Church of Glasgow. Another Gavin Hamilton (1751–1805) was a staunch friend of the poet Burns, who included in his Kilmarnock edition of 1786, 'A Dedication to G**** H******** Esq'. Gavin Maxwell (1914–69) was the author of *Ring of Bright Water* and other best-sellers. The name Gavin was much used by the gypsies of southern Scotland, and there is a village in Berwickshire called Gavinton, built at the instance of David Gavin of Langton in 1760. Gaven, which appears as a surname in Caithness, may have a different origin: perhaps the Gaelic *gobhainn*, a smith. Other variants are Gawain and Gavine.

GEMMA (f) It is probable that in early times this name was a feminine form of James or Jaime, but in the nineteenth century it became associated with the Italian *gemma*, 'a gem'. It was borne by St Gemma [Galganil] (1875–1903) and has been favoured by Roman Catholic families. It is about twentieth in popularity for girls' names.

GEOFFREY (m) O.G. *gud-frid*, 'good peace'. It was identified at an early period with *Gottfried* or *Gaufried* (GODFREY), which in many cases it must have been. An early bearer of the name was Godfrey, brother of Count Eustace of Boulogne. He took part in the first Crusade and in 1099 became Defender of the Holy Sepulchre at Jerusalem. Maud, Queen of David I of Scotland had a cousin named Geoffrey. The Latinised forms included

Galfrius and Geoffridus, and gave rise to surnames such as Geoffrey, Geoffreys, Jeffrey, Jeffries and possibly Giffin. As a forename it has been well used. Galfrid Melville settled in Scotland before 1162, and was ancestor of the Melville earls. Geoffrey Blund was the first recorded burgess of Inverness, *c.* 1200. The surname is the feudal Blount. Geoffrey (Galfredus) was postulated Bishop of Dunkel in 1236, but was disallowed by the Pope. One of the finest medievalists of modern times is Geoffrey Wallis Steuart Barrow, emeritus Professor of Scottish History and Palaeography at the University of Edinburgh. Pet forms are Geoff and Jeff, the latter sometimes a forename in its own right. The Gaelic form is *Goiridh.*

GEORGE (m) Gr. *Georgios* 'husbandman'. St George, patron saint of England, was a Roman military tribune martyred in 303, and remembered by the crusaders who brought his cult back to England. The name came to Scotland in the fourteenth century. George, 10th Earl of Dunbar, born *c.* 1340, was followed by George, 11th and last earl. George Lauder was Bishop of Argyll in 1389. The name is said to have occurred in the northern family of Munro before 1340, but proof is lacking. With the accession to the throne of Britain by the House of Hanover in 1714, and 116 years of unbroken succession of sovereigns of the name to 1830, the name became firmly established. In the present century George V reigned 1910–36, and George VI 1936–52. A 'Geordie' is the name given to Northumbrians, and in Scotland is a pet name, as is Dod and Doddie. The

Gaelic form of the name is *Deorsa*, and the usual feminine form is GEORGINA.

GEORGINA (f) In Scotland the feminine form of GEORGE has been in use since the early eighteenth century. Georgina Caroline (1727–1809) was a daughter of Henry Scott of Deloraine. Georgina, daughter of the Hon Marie Murray Hay-Mackenzie and Edward Hay of Newhall, married James [Boyle], Earl of Glasgow in 1821. Variants are Georgiana, Georgia and Georgine. Gina is a pet name.

GERALD (m) O. Ger. *ger-vald*, 'spear', and 'rule', giving *Gairovald*, sometimes taken to mean 'spear-wielder'. The name came to England with the Conqueror in 1066, and was in frequent use throughout the Middle Ages. There was a mid-nineteenth century revival, when Gerald became more fashionable than GERARD. Variant spellings recorded include Gerrald, Gerrold, Jerald and Jerold. Pet forms are Gerry and Jerry. The feminine form is GERALDINE.

GERALDINE (f) The feminine form of GERALD has been in use at least since the early sixteenth century. Its use has increased since Geraldine Chaplin, born 1944, played a part in the film *Doctor Zhivago* (1965), but the name is still outwith the top one hundred girls' names registered annually in Scotland.

GERARD (m) O.G. *ger-ard*, 'strong with the spear'. The name was well used in the Middle Ages and probably came to Britain with the Normans. Sir Gerard de Lindsay of Luffness died in 1249, and the name appears in a later generation of the Lindsays. At one period the name was often confused with GERALD, and, after a revival in the nineteenth century, that name became more popular. There is a French feminine form, Gerardine, but it is uncommon. Gerry and Jerry are pet names.

GERTRUDE (f) O.G. 'spear-maiden'. In Norse mythology, Gertrude was the name of one of the Valkyries or Rhine maidens: the goddesses who transported those killed in battle to Valhalla (the place of bliss). The name may have come to Britain from Holland, where a seventh-century saint was revered. It appears in various forms in the Middle Ages but stabilised as Gertrude. Sir Walter Aston (1583–1639), Baron of Forfar, married *c.* 1607, Gertrude, daughter of Sir Thomas Sadlier of Standon, Herts, whose second wife was Gertrude Markham. They had a daughter Gertrude who died in infancy, and they named another girl Gertrude. The Scots poet Thomas Campbell popularised the name with his *Gertrude of Wyoming* (1809). Although not now prolific, the name has been borne by some celebrities, including the actress Gertrude Lawrence (1898–1952). Pet forms are Gert, Gertie, Trudie and Jerry.

GIDEON (m) Heb. meaning 'hewer'. In the Bible it is the name of the son of Joash and one of the judges of Israel. He delivered Israel from the Midianites who, with the Amelekites, were ravaging the country (OT, Judges 7:1–7; 8:11–28). The name appeared in Scotland before the Reformation and came into regular, if not common, use. Gideon, son of Andrew Murray of Blackbarony, was born *c.* 1555, and in his minority had a charter of the lands of Glenpoit in Ettrick Forrest erected with others into a barony in 1601. In Scott's *Woodstock*, Gibbet was a pet name given by Bletson to his secretary, Gideon, and in *The Heart of Midlothian*, the novelist has Gideon Sharpitlaw as Procurator Fiscal. The Gideons are a modern international body which *inter alia* places bibles in hotel rooms and hospitals.

GILBERT (m) O.G. *gisil*, 'pledge', and *berhta*, 'bright'. The name was known to the Anglo-Saxons as *Eormengild*. It increased numerically after the Conquest and gave rise to the surnames Gibb, Gibson, Gibbieson and Gibbonson. Andrew, Bishop of Caithness in 1164, had a brother Gilbert, who received a charter of the lands of Monogrum (Monorgan) in Angus, from David, brother of William the Lion, confirmed by the king. The ancestor of the ancient earls of Galloway was Gilbert, Earl of Orkney and Caithness, who died in 1256. Among famous Scots who have borne the name was Dr Gilbert Burnett (1643–1715), historian and divine. Burns enthusiasts will recall the poet's staid brother, Gilbert (1760–1827). Sir Walter Scott has Gilbert of Lockswood in his *Ivanhoe*. In *The Fair Maid of Perth*, Gilbert is butler to Sir Patrick Charteris. Scott has also Gilbert of Cranberry Moor as a landowner in the *Monastery*. The name is not now so popular. In Gaelic it is rendered *Gillebard* or *Gillebride*. Pet names are Gib, Gibbie, Gil, Geb and Gebbie.

GILCHRIST (m) Gael. 'servant of Christ'. The exquisite St Martin's cross in Iona was the work of a sculptor of this name. It bears the inscription in old Irish

characters: *Oroit do Gillacrist doringal t[-in] chros
sa*. The name is also recorded in *The Book of Deer*
before 1132, and is found in the families of the Earls
of Lennox and Earls of Mar. In some cases the name
has been Anglicised as CHRISTOPHER. Moreover, in
much the same way the surname Christie is occasionally derived.

GILES (m, f) Gr. *aigidion*, 'young goat', Latinised
Egidius (feminine EGIDIA). St Giles (Eegidius) was
the Athenian who took his name from the goatskin
he wore as a shield. He went to France, where he was
called Giles, perhaps from the Celtic *gille* (servant),
because of his humility. St Giles is the patron saint
of beggars and cripples. The name came to Britain
after the Conquest, and in Scotland both the masculine and feminine forms were in use. Many churches
were dedicated to St Giles, including the High Kirk of
Edinburgh. Nowadays, when Giles is found, it is usually
masculine. Scott makes use of the name in *The Bride
of Lammermoor, Ivanhoe, The Fortunes of Nigel* and
The Pirate. See also JULIA.

GILLEAN (m) Gael. 'servant of St John'. Some old pedi-
grees derive the descent of several Highland clans
from Gilleoin of the Aird (west of Inverness), notably
Clann Ainnrais (Gillanders), the Mathesons and the
MacKenzies. Gilleoin is difficult to date, but lived
before another Gilleoin, the eponymous ancestor of the
MacLeans, probably alive in the reign of Alexander III
(1249–86). The name appears in the genealogy of the
MacNeils. Gillieonan was chief of that clan, *c.* 1427,

and was succeeded by his son of the same name. Early use as a surname led to names such as Gilzean.

GILLIAN (f) Lat. a form of GILES and JULIA, earlier EGIDIA. Forms of the name were used in the Middle Ages, but Gillian evolved to become uncommon in the late eighteenth century. It was revived in comparatively recent times. Sir Walter Scott has Dame Gillian as a 'comely, middle-aged woman' in *The Betrothed* (1825). Recorded variants are Gillianne, Gillyanne and Jillianne. Pet forms are Gill and especially JILL, which is often used independently.

GILLIES (m) Gael. *Gille Iosa*, 'servant of Jesus'. The name has displaced the older MALISE, *Maol Iosa*, 'tonsured servant', a name favoured anciently by the Grahams. Gillies, Gillis and Gilles were popular variants in the Western Isles and in Strathspey. Gillise was witness to the charter by David I to the Abbey of Holyrood, *c.* 1128. Gylis, son of Angus the shoemaker, did homage to the Prior of St Andrews at Dull in 1264. Some eighteenth-century Macphersons in Badenoch bore Gilies as a forename, and it was anglicised as ELIAS. Many families with the surname Gillies and Gillis emigrated to Canada before 1867.

GODFREY (m) O.G., *Guda*, 'God', *frithu*, 'peace'. Usually interpreted as 'God's Peace'. It probably came to Britain with the Normans, and replaced an earlier O.E. name, *Godfrith*. John Godfrason witnessed a quit-claim of the lands of Gladsmuir, East Lothian, in 1427. He was probably the John Gothrasoun, serjeant to the sheriff in 1430. In Gaelic the name is rendered

Guaidhre or *Goraidh*, and gave rise to the surnames Gorrie, MacGorrie and MacGorry. At one period the name was frequently confused with GEOFFREY.

GORDON (m) This is another example of a surname in regular use as a forename. People who arrived in Scotland after the Norman Conquest settled in Berwickshire and took their name from a place named Gordon, probably *gordun*, 'hill-fort'. They came to own lands in Galloway and also in Strathbogie. By marriage they gained Aboyne. The Gordons Earls of Huntly were called 'Cock o' the North'. There was a famous regiment, the Gordon Highlanders, amalgamated in 1994 with the Queen's Highlanders to form the Highlanders. General Charles Gordon (1833–85), of Khartoum fame, gave the name immense standing, and as a forename it is now very popular.

GRACE (f) Lat. *gratia*, 'grace' or 'favour'. Although found in fourth-century Rome, the name was not popular in Britain until favoured by the Puritans, who took it to America. In Scotland it was well used, but in many cases derived from Grizel, shortened to Gris and softened to Grace. Indeed, in Gaelic, Grace is rendered *Giorsail*. Grace Johnston, niece of Gordon of Balmaghie, became mistress of her uncle, Murray of Broughton, before 1790. The heroine Grace Darling (1815–42), probably contributed to the popularity of the name.

GRAHAM, GRAEME (m) As a surname Graham derives from Grantham, in Lincolnshire, and early members of the family may have come from Flanders or Normandy. William de Graham accompanied David I (1124–53) from England to Scotland, and received from him the lands of Dalkeith and Abercorn. The Grahams played an active part in the War of Independence. Although not strictly a Highland Clan, the Grahams came to own land along the 'Highland Line', and the Duke of Montrose is chief of the family. The name came gradually into use as a forename, and is popular today, with variants Grahame and Graeme, the latter highly favoured.

GRANT (m) A surname used also as a Christian name. The original meaning was 'tall' from the French *le grand*. The Clan Grant are especially associated with Strathspey, and were probably of Norman extraction. Sir Lawrence le Grant was Sheriff of Inverness in 1263–64. The surname has produced some notable people, including Mrs Elizabeth Grant (1799–1885) of Rothiemurchus, the author, Sir Francis J. Grant (1863–1953), Lord Lyon and Dr Isabel F. Grant (1887–1983), historian and folklorist. The use as a forename appears to have commenced in the USA, and was probably influenced by the 18th President, Ulysses S. Grant (1822–85). Dr Grant G. Simpson is a retired senior lecturer in Scottish History at the University of Aberdeen.

GREG (m) This is a surname which has come into use as a forename. Occasionally it is a short form of GREGOR. The name appears also as Greig, Grieg, Grig and Grige. Walter Greg witnessed a charter by Malcolm, Earl of Fife, between 1214 and 1226. Patrick Grige was admitted burgess of Aberdeen in 1488, and David

Greg was a council member at Stirling in 1522. The Norwegian composer, Edvard Grieg (1843–1907), was a great-grandson of Alexander Greg, who emigrated to Norway in the 1750s. Admiral Greig (1735–88), creator of the Russian navy, was a Scot. Use as a forename is fairly modern, but Greg is now within the top one hundred boys' names. The variant Gregg is not high in favour.

GREGOR (m) Lat. *gregorus*, 'watchful', and rendered *Gregorius*. It is an early form of GREGORY. The MacGregors descend from Gregor of the Golden Bridles, who lived in the fourteenth century, and whose son, Ian *Cam*, held the homelands of Glenorchy, Glenstrae and Strathfillan. The name came to be used as a forename, and is now quite fashionable.

GREGORY (m) An early form of a post-biblical name, prolific in the Roman Empire. No less than sixteen popes have borne the name, the earliest being Gregory the Great in 590. Gregorius was seneschal of Coldingham Priory during the reign of William the Lion. Many ecclesiastics bore the name in the twelfth and thirteenth centuries. The Gaels rendered the short form of GREGOR, as *Griogair*. The late Gregory Peck, the film actor, has probably contributed to the popularity of the name.

GRIZEL, GRIZELDA (m) O.G. probably meaning 'grey battle-maiden'. It is possible the name had some early association with Italy. Boccaccio told of a wife whose patience was sorely tried by her husband in the *Decameron*, and Chaucer re-told the tale. Griselda was a much used form, and in the later Middle Ages became associated with patience. Grizel, variously spelt Grizzel, Girsel, Girzel and Goirzel, was popular in Scotland. It was borne by nobility and commoners alike. A notable woman of the name was Grisell (1665–1746), daughter of the 1st Earl of Marchmont, whose mother and maternal grandmother both bore the name. She married George Baillie of Jerviswood in 1692. Lady Baillie wrote several Scottish songs, and her *Household Book* (1692–1733) was printed by the Scottish History Society in 1911. In Scotland Grizel often became GRACE.

GWENDOLEN (f) Welsh *gwen*, 'fair' and *dolen*, 'ring, bow'. Often given as 'white-browed'. Guendoloena, daughter of Corineus, and wife of Lochrin, son of Brute, is legendary. The name was used in the 1860s and became more popular after publication of the novel *Daniel Deronda*, by George Eliot (Mary Ann Cross, née Evans, 1819–80). Variants are Gwendoline, Gwendolyn, Gwendolene and Gwendolyn. The short form is Gwen.

H

HAMISH (m) An anglicised form of the vocative case of the Gaelic *Seumas* – James, and sometimes used independently. In Scott's *The Highland Widow*, Hamish

MacTavish is 'a daring cateran' called MacTavish *Mhor*. Hamish appears frequently as a pet name rather than as an alternative for James.

HANNA, HANNAH (f) Heb. *Hanani*, 'favoured one'. The biblical Hanna was the wife of Elhanak and mother of Samuel (OT, 1 Samuel 1:2). Hannah, daughter of Anthony Haig of Bemersyde, 'the Quaker', married James Dickson of Belchester in 1729. In Scott's *St Ronan's Well*, Hannah is Mr Bindloose's housekeeper, and in *Redgauntlet*, Hannah is Mr Saunders Fairfield's housekeeper 'unparalleled for cleanliness among the women of Auld Reekie'. Sometimes Hannah is a pet name for JOHANNA. Hannah is still a fashionable name; it is within the top thirty girls' names, but the variant Hanna is not prolific. Diminutives are ANN and ANNA.

HAROLD (m) O.E *here*, 'host' and *weald*, 'power', often stated as giving *Hereweald*, 'army wielder'. There is a corresponding O.Nor. *Harivald*, later Harald, and it was known among the Anglo-Danes. Harald Maddadson, Earl, granted to the Roman See, a penny yearly from every inhabited house in Caithness, *c*. 1181. Haraldus was Bishop of Argyll, 1200–03. In our time, Harold MacMillan (1894–1986), descended from Arran crofters, was Prime Minister of Great Britain, 1957–63, and in 1984 was created Earl of Stockton.

HARRIET (f) This is an English form of the French Henriette, a feminine form of HENRY or HARRY. The French form often became Henrietta. It is said to have been introduced to Britain by Henriette Marie, daughter of Henri IV of France and Mary de Medici, who became the wife of Charles I in 1625. Harriot was a popular form. Harriot, a younger daughter of George Hamilton, MP for Donegal, 1727–60, married the Rev. William Peter, and died in 1787. The name appears in several branches of the Hamiltons, including the Earls of Abercorn. The Gaelic form is *Eiric*. Pet names are Hattie, Hatty and Hetty.

HARRY (m) A common form of HENRY, especially in Scotland, where it often appears as Harie and Harrie. Harry Cheape of West Pitcairnie, Perthshire, figured in the Raid of Ruthven, 1582. In 1611, Harrie Ruthven was Tutor of Ruthven. Harry Gordon of Avochi took part in the 1715 Jacobite Rising.

HARVEY (m) Fr. *Herve*, from the Celtic *haer*, 'strong' and *ber*, 'ardent'. *Herve* was a Breton personal name, meaning 'battle-worthy'. The name came to Scotland about a century after the Norman Conquest. Hervey, also called HERBERT, obtained the lands of Keith in East Lothian, which were called Harvey-Keith, later Keith-Marischal. His son Malcolm witnessed a charter to the monks of Kelso in 1185. He died in his father's lifetime, and his grandson, another Hervey, confirmed a grant by Symon Fraser to the monks. They were ancestors of the Keiths, Earl Marischals of Scotland. The name gave rise to the surnames Harvey, Harvie, Hervie and Harveson. The modern use as a forename is simply due to wide use as a surname.

HAYLEY (f) Found as a surname in England as early as 1225, the name probably means 'dweller by the hay land', or meadow. The modern use as a forename is probably due to the actress Hayley Mills, whose career began about 1959. It is now among the top fifty girls' names, and recorded variants are Haley, Hailey, Halie, Haylee and Hayleigh.

HAZEL (f) A tree name which came into use as a forename in the latter part of the nineteenth century. Variants recorded in different countries are Hazell, Hazelle and Hazal, with occasional extended forms such as Hazeline and Hazelgrove.

HEATHER (f) A plant name which also came into use in the nineteenth century, and is now within the top forty girls' names registered annually in Scotland.

HECTOR (m) Gr., 'holding fast'. This was the name of the Trojan hero who was slain by the Greek Achilles. 'Sir Ector' was a hero of popular literature in the later Middle Ages, and the name took root in the Scottish Highlands, where it came to be used as an equivalent for *Eachan*, a Gaelic name totally unconnected. Hector Boece (1465–1536) was a Scottish historian. He was a good Latinist but rather credulous. Alexander Forbes of Pitsligo, who died in 1562, had a son Hector. Hector Abercrombie, grandfather of Lord Glassford, had a charter of the lands of Westhalls, Aberdeenshire, in 1590. Hector was a favourite name among the MacLeans of the West Highlands.

HELEN, HELENA (f) Gr., 'bright one'. The use of the name, although it appears on early Christian inscriptions, is largely due to St Helena (died AD 338), mother of the Emperor Constantine the Great. The name is found as AILEEN, EILEEN, ELAINE and ELEANOR. The 'H' probably came in at the Renaissance, when the study of classical literature brought Homer's story of the Trojan war and the Greek Queen Helen to public notice. The variant Helena is often used, also Ellen. Helen Craik (1750–1825) of the Arbigland family, was a spinster novelist and versifier known to Robert Burns. The old haunting ballad, 'Fair Helen of Kir[k]connell', in Scott's *Minstrelsy of the Scottish Border* (1802–3), kept the name popular in the Scottish countryside. The lady was Helen Irving or Bell, and her suitor was Adam Fleming, killed by a rival after Helen had died shielding him. The Gaelic form of the name is Eilidh. Pet names are Ella, Nell, Nellie and Nelly.

HENRIETTA *See* HARRIET.

HENRY (m) O.G. *haimi*, 'house' and *ric*, 'ruler', giving 'head of a household'. In German the name was rendered *Haimirich* or *Heinrich*, and in French became *Henri*. The name appears on record in Scotland in the twelfth century and gave rise to the surnames Hendrie, Hendry and Henry. In its Latin form it appears in the twelfth century. Henricus, the steward, was a witness, *c.* 1185, and Henricus Le Cheyne was elected Bishop of Aberdeen in 1282. Heinrekr or Henry, a canon of Orkney, became bishop there in 1248. Hal, Harie and HARRY are popular variants in Scotland, and the name gave rise to the surname Henryson. Hal o' the Wynd fought in the famous clan battle on the Inch at Perth in 1396. Henry Dundas (1742–1811) was for nearly thirty years the most powerful man in Scotland.

Torphichen-born Henry Bell (1767–1830) was a pioneer in steamboat power, and Henry Raeburn (1756–1823) of Edinburgh was a famous portrait painter who was knighted in 1822. The names Henry and Harry are still well used.

HERBERT (m) O.G. *harja*, 'host', and *berhta*, 'bright', usually interpreted as 'illustrious army'. There was a corresponding O.E. word, *Herebeorht*, but not widely used. The name was re-introduced after the Conquest and became quite prolific in Scotland. Herbert de Maccuswell, ancestor of the Maxwells, Earls of Nithsdale, appears on record in 1200, and the name occurs in later generations of the family. Sir Herbert Eustace Maxwell (1845–1937) of Monreith, 7th baronet, was a noted historian and politician. The name is known also as a surname, and among those who influenced its use was Welsh hymn-writer George Herbert (1593–1633). Diminutives of the forename are Herb, Herbie and Bertie.

HERCULES (m) Gr., meaning 'Glory of Hera', who was queen of the Olympian goddesses. Hercules is a Latin form of the name of the Greek hero remembered for his twelve great feats of strength. The Jewish Hercules was Samson who died *c.* 1113 BC. The name has appeared sporadically in Scotland, and in the Shetland Isles has appeared as equivalent to the Norwegian Hakon. Hercules, son of Sir Robert Carnegie of Kinnaird, died in 1565. Hercules Stewart of Whitelaw, natural brother of Francis, Earl of Bothwell, is on record in 1593. Bervie-born Hercules Linton (1837–1900) was associated with the building of the famous sailing ship the *Cutty Sark*. Crime writer Agatha Christie (1890–1976) made the fictional Belgian detective Hercule Poirot a celebrity worthy of a TV series.

HESTER *See* ESTHER

HEW *See* HUGH

HILARY (m, f) Lat. *hilarus*, 'cheerful'. St Hilarius of Poitiers, who died in 368, defended the church in France against Arianism. Another St Hilarius was Pope, 461–68. The name spread to Ireland, and Elarius, a scribe of Lochra, Tipperary, is on record in 810. The Gaelic form became *Ealair*, and the surname MacElair became MacKellar, a common Argyll name. The name was used for males and females until the seventeenth century, after which it was given to girls. In France it appears as *Hilaire*. The name is still in use in Scotland, where occasionally it appears as Hillary.

HILDA (f) O.Ger., and one of many names beginning with *hilde*, 'battle', and thought to mean 'battle maiden'. The venerable Bede records the death of Abbess Hilda at Streanasalch [Whitby] in 680, aged 66. When names of Anglo-Saxon saints were revived by the Tractarians in the nineteenth century, Hilda became popular. Hilda Rose Montgomerie, daughter of Archibald, 13th Earl of Eglinton, was born in 1860. In Scott's *Ivanhoe*, Hilda of Middleham is Prior Aymer's 'respected grandmother'.

HOLLY (f) A plant name used as a forename. It came into use at the beginning of this century. It seems probable that Galsworthy's use of the name in *The Forsythe*

Saga has contributed to its popularity, especially since the TV series of that name. Variants are Holli, Hollie and Holley.

HOMER (m) Gr., meaning 'hostage pledge'. Homer was the Greek poet to whom are attributed the great epics, the *Iliad* and the *Odyssey*, written 850–800 BC. The name has never been fashionable in Scotland, but occurs as early as the fifteenth century. Homer, son of John, 3rd Lord Maxwell, who died in 1484, had a son Homer, progenitor of the Maxwells of Portrack. The name was also used by the Flesher family of Dumfries in the seventeenth century.

HUGH (m) O.G. *hugu*, 'mind' or 'spirit'. The name was introduced to Britain by the Normans. Count Hugh de Montfort-sur-Risle fought at Hastings in 1066. The name soon spread to Scotland. Hugh, chaplain to King William the Lion, was intruded as bishop of St Andrews in 1178, and the monarch consented to his consecration. A papal legate was sent to inquire, and John, called 'the Scott', although by birth English, was consecrated bishop in 1180. Another Hugh, son of a priest, became bishop of Brechin in 1214. Hugh, 4th Earl of Ross, succeeded his father in 1323, and married Matilda, daughter of Robert the Bruce. By his second wife, Margaret Graham, he had a son Hugh, first of Balnagowan. The name remained in favour and from it evolved the surnames Hughson, Houston, Hughes, Hugget, Hewitt and Jewlett. Hugh is the accepted English equivalent of the Gaelic *Aodh*, but there is no connection in origin or meaning. In the West Highlands

Hugh is recognised as the English equivalent of *Eòghan* (see EUGÉNE), and in other areas is an anglicised form of *Uisdeann*. The late Christopher Murray Grieve, one of Scotland's literary giants, wrote under the name of Hugh MacDiarmid. Pet forms of Hugh are Hughie, Shug and Shuggie. The Latin form, HUGO, has been used in Scotland. The old feminine form Hughina is not now favoured.

HUGO (m) A form of HUGH which has declined in popularity. Hugo Arnot (1749–86), son of a Leith shipmaster, wrote a *History of Edinburgh* (1779), and complied *Ancient Criminal Trials* (1785). Of great height and extraordinarily thin, he was satirised by the caricaturist John Kay.

HUMPHREY (m) O.G. *hun-frid*, 'great for peace'. The name came to Scotland in the later Middle Ages and appears as both forename and surname. Andrew Umfray, Dean of Dunkeld, was Bishop Elect there and died at Rome *c.* 1378. Umfridus de Kilpatrick had a grant of the lands of Colquhoun, Dumbartonshire, *c.* 1240. The name Humphrey appears in later generations of that family. Umphryd Jerdyn of Applegirth is on record about 1390. In Gaelic the Colquhouns are called *Mac a' Chounich*. The surname Umphreyson is simply 'son of Umphrey'. A variant spelling is Umpherson. Little Beatrix Umpherson and other children in Pentland village near Edinburgh, signed a covenant now known as *The Children's Band* in 1683. Either she or a later Beatrix Umpherson married John McNeil at Pentland in 1708.

I

IAIN (m) Gael. for JOHN, often rendered Eoin and Ian. A poem addressed to Eoin mac Suibhne on his setting out from Ulster in 1310 to claim his ancestral lands of Knapdale, has 'hail at the streams of Sliabh Monaidh to MacSuibhne of Sliabh Mis'. Eoin, ancestor of the MacLeans who settled in Mull, flourished c. 1330. 'Ian Lom' (Bald John), or John MacDonald (1620–1710), was a Gaelic poet and clan bard. In recent times, Sir Iain Moncreiffe of that Ilk (1919–1985) was a brilliant genealogist and armorist. The form Iain is more popular today than Ian, and is within the top forty boys' names registered annually.

IDA (f) O.G. *id*, equivalent to the O.Nor. *idh*, 'labour'. Ida, the daughter of the Duke of Bas Lorraine, married Eustace II, Count of Boulogne, and died c. 1113. The name was brought to England after the Norman Conquest. It appears also as a pet name for old names beginning with Ida. Idania, daughter of William Gurley, Lord of Fritht, is called Ida in some documents relating to the lands of Stanhus in the Lordship of Dunipace, c. 1296. The name faded after the fourteenth century, but made a revival in the nineteenth. Ida is the heroine of Tennyson's poem, 'The Princess' (1874). The British-born film actress and director Ida Lupino died in 1995.

IDONEA (f) Possibly from O.Nor. *Idhuna*, a goddess of

spring, associated with *idh*, 'labour' (see also IDA). The name appears in England in the twelfth century, and came early to Scotland. Idonea Comyn, daughter of William, Earl of Buchan, married Sir Gilbert Hay before 1233. She was named after her paternal aunt, Idonea of Auchtercoul, in Mar, who married Sir Adam Fitz Gilbert. Idonea, sister of Sir Henry Graham of Dalkeith, married Sir Adam Swinburne before 1291. The name did not become common as a forename but the surnames Ednay, Idney and Idden derive from it.

IONA (f) The name derives from the island of Iona, off Mull, where St Columba founded a monastery in 563. It is in regular, but quiet use.

IRENE (f) Gr., *Eirene*, 'peace', Latinised Irene. This was a common forename in the time of the Roman Empire. There was a fourth-century saint of that name. It does not appear to have been much used in Britain until around the middle of the nineteenth century. The Empress Irene, wife of Alexius Comnenus in Scott's *Count Robert of Paris*, admired the accomplishments of her daughter Comnean. The name is still in use in Scotland, but is not prolific. Pet forms are Rena, Renie, Rene and Renee, all of which have been used independently.

ISAAC (m) Heb. *yishag*, 'laughter'. The name of the son of ABRAHAM and SARAH, born when she was past normal child-bearing age (OT, Genesis 21:1–6). It was not uncommon among churchmen of the twelfth and thirteenth centuries. Isaac was prior of Scone, 1154–62, and Magister Isaac was a cleric of St Andrews, 1201.

Isaac, burgess of Aberbrothoc, witnessed a charter by MATILDA, Countess of Angus, *c.* 1242. Andrew Isak had a safe conduct into England in 1405. Probably the most famous person to bear the name was Sir Isaac Newton (1642–1727), who described the laws of motion and gravity. The name came to be used as a Gaelic surname, *MacIosaig*, anglicised as McIsaac. The name has been in regular use for centuries, but lost favour during the Second World War, when it was thought to be Jewish. Pet forms are Ik, Ike, Ikey, and occasionally Zac, which it shares with ZACHARY.

ISABEL, ISOBEL (f) This is a Spanish-Portuguese rendering of ELIZABETH, and probably came to Scotland from France, where Isabelle is used. Derived from Isabeau and Ilsabeth. Robert de Brus, who died in 1245, styled 'The Noble', married Isabel, daughter of David, Earl of Huntingdon, of the blood royal. It was through her that their grandson Robert 'the Competitor' claimed the crown of Scotland in 1292. His mother was Isobel, natural daughter of William the Lion. Robert married Marjorie, daughter of Neil, Earl of Carrick, and their son Robert became King of Scots in 1306. Edward Bruce, Earl of Carrick, and brother of Robert I, married Isabel, daughter of John, Earl of Atholl. The name remained in constant use. The famous opera singer Isobel Baillie (1895–1983) was a native of Hawick. Variant spellings are Isabella, Isobella, and Ishbel, the latter derived from the Gaelic *Iseabal*. Pet forms of the name are Bell, Bella, Lalla, Ib and Isa. Occasionally Tibby appears and Shibby, which is more common in Ireland. The surnames Isabel, Isbell, Ibbs, Ibson, Ibbitson and Ibbotson, all derive from Isabel or Isobel.

ISLA (f) A forename derived from a river and glen in Perthshire. It is modern and owes much to the TV personality, Isla St Clair, and also to the actress Isla Blair, who have kept the name before the public.

IVAR (m) O.Nor. A personal name, *Ivarr*, the meaning of which is obscure. It was borne by several Danish kings of Dublin in the ninth and tenth centuries and was borrowed by the Gaels, who rendered it *Imhaer* and *Iomhar*. The name was brought to Argyll and Yver Campbell appears as laird of Strachur in 1330. His descendants came to be called MacIver Campbells. Elsewhere in the Highlands and Western Isles, the name was in common use both as forename and surname. Variants are Iver and Ivor. The *Slioch Nan*, or race of Ivor, is mentioned by Scott in *Waverley*. Ivar Dhu Campbell features prominently in Ivory Burnett's novel, *The Ravens Enter the House* (1931). See also EVANDER.

IVY (m, f) Said to be a plant name introduced *c.* 1860, and for girls. However it was in use as a masculine name in the West of Scotland as early as the seventeenth century. Ivie Haire (1640–91) of Rankinson, Coylton parish, Ayrshire, was buried at Alloway. The name appears in later generations of the family, who came to spell the surname Hair, then Hare and rendered the forename Ivy. Ivie Boyd (1759–1825) was also interred at Alloway. The name is possibly cognate with the O.G. *Ivo*, from *Iv*, 'yew', but appears occasionally as a pet name for IVAR.

J

JACK (m) Nowadays Jack is a variant of JOHN, but more correctly JAMES, from the French *Jacques*, pronounced 'zhak'. As early as 1453 it appears as a forename, when Jak Donaldson in Coupar Grange is on record. Jack Richardson is recorded in 1469. As a surname, Jack appears in 1480, when Duncan Jak was a charter witness at Dundee. Robert Jack, merchant-burgess of Dundee was hanged and quartered in 1567, for uttering false coin brought from Flanders. The surname Jackson is simply 'son of Jack'. Jack is now used independently as a boys' name (see also JOCK). 'Every man Jack' is a common term for every individual, hence 'Jack of all trades'.

JACOBINA (f) Feminine form of James or Jacob (Latinised *Jacobus*). Sir John Hamilton of Cadzow married Jacoba, daughter of Sir James Douglas of Dalkeith, *c.* 1388. The form Jacobina was much in use by families involved in the Jacobite risings of 1715 and 1745.

JACQUELINE (f) Fr. and derived from the feminine form of Jacques (James or Jacob), introduced possibly from Belgium in the fourteenth century. Jacquetta is also derived from the French name. There are numerous variants, including Jacquelyn, Jacqui, Jackalyn, Jacquiline and Jacqulynn. Jack and Jackie are short forms. The American actress Jacqueline Bissett, born 1946, star of *The Grasshopper* and other films, has probably influenced the use of the name, which is within the top seventy-five names for girls in Scotland.

JADE (f) A modern forename derived from the precious stone. Up to the middle of the present century there was a word 'yade' or 'yad', which meant a worn-out horse, and this contemptuous term was occasionally used to describe a woman; similar to hussy. Jade is becoming a popular name, and the variant Jayde has been recorded.

JAMES (m) The name developed from the Latin *Jacobus*. Two of the twelve apostles of Jesus Christ were called James. They were James 'the Great', son of Zebedee, and James, son of Alphaeus. There was a third James, called 'The Less', supposed to be a brother of Jesus. James 'the Great' and PETER belonged to an inner circle among the apostles. The fact that James, son of Alphaeus, is not mentioned by JOHN, lends strength to the belief that the gospel attributed to him was written by later theologians. The name was in use in the Middle Ages. James, elected Bishop of Caithness by the chapter *c.* 1294, was not canonically celebrated, and the Pope declared the appointment null. The name was more highly favoured after the late fourteenth century, and there were seven kings of the name – James I, reigned 1406–37; James II, 1437–60; James III, 1460–88; James IV, 1488–1513; James VI, 1513–42; James VI of Scotland from the abdication of his mother, Mary, Queen of Scots, in 1567, and I of England, 1603–25; James VII and II, 1625–88 (with intervals). The Old Pretender, James, son of James VII and II, and his second wife, Mary of Modena, was called VIII and III by the Jacobites. By 1864 James had become the second-most popular name in Scotland; today it is within the top ten most favoured names. The name JAMIE is now frequently used independently. In Gaelic James is rendered *Sheumas* or *Seumas* (see also HAMISH). Some famous Scots have borne the Christian name of James. These include James Hutton (1726–97), pioneer geologist, James Watt (1736–1819), pioneer of steam condensing, and James M. Barrie (1860–1937), a prolific writer and portrayer of Scottish life. Pet forms are Jim, Jimac, Jimmy, JAMIE, Jamesie, and at one time JACK. Feminine forms are Jamesina (not now in favour), Jametta, Jamelia and Jamell.

JAMIE (m, f) Popular form of JAMES, and now the most favoured feminine form, perhaps influenced by Jamie Lee Curtis, the American actress.

JAN See JANET

JANE (f) A prolific feminine form of JOHN, Latinised JOHANNA. The Gaelic form is SINE or SIONA. In Scotland, many girls registered as Jane are called JEAN. Like JANET, Jean is also used independently. The most celebrated Jane in Scottish history was Lady Jane Douglas (1698–1753) who married Col John Stewart of Grandtully. When she was forty-eight years old she is said to have had twin sons born in France, named Sholto and Archibald. This triggered off the great legal wrangle known as 'The Douglas Cause', for succession to the estates of the 3rd Marquess of Douglas, decided by the House of Lords in 1779 in favour of Archibald

Douglas. There is a great body of printed material regarding the case, including the historical novel *The Heir of Douglas (1953)*, by Lillian de la Torre. Another well-known Scottish lady was Jane Ferrier (1767–1846), sister of the novelist Susan Ferrier. A clever artist, she met the poet Burns, who sent her some verses. Modern variants of Jane include Jayne, Jaine, Janine and JENNY.

JANET (f) Originally a diminutive form of JANE, the name became popular in its own right, but grew less fashionable about the middle of the last century. Janet, daughter of Sir John Stewart of Balvany, 2nd Earl of Atholl, married Alexander Gordon, Master of Sutherland, in 1520. Many women christened Janet are called JESSIE. The Gaelic form is *Seonaid*. In Scott's novel *The Fortunes of Nigel*, Janet is a laundress who had been a 'faithful drudge' to Margaret Ramsay. Old registers have the name often as Jonet. Janetta is a modern form. Pet forms of the name are Jan, Janie, Jenn, Jennie and JENNY.

JASON (m) Gr. *Eason*, by some authorities 'a healer', and cognate with the Hebrew Joshua. Jason was a celebrated hero of antiquity and son of Aeson, King of Iolcos. To gain the restoration of his father's kingdom from Pelias, he undertook the search for the Golden Fleece, aided by Media (whom he married but later deserted) and the Argonauts. He accomplished his mission. However the forename is derived from the scriptural Jason, who lived in Thessalonica. PAUL and Silas resided with him. His home was attacked by an anti-Christian mob.

Jason is generally accepted as the author of the book of *Ecclesiasticus*. The name was not much in use until the present century and has been influenced by actors and films. Several actors have borne the name. Jason Robards acted in silent films, and his better-known son of the same name, born at Chicago in 1922, has appeared in Eugene O'Neill's plays and in films, including the remake of *Inherit the Wind*. The name was given a boost by the film *Jason and the Argonauts* (1963). The Scottish film star Sir Sean Connery has a son Jason.

JASPER (m) This is the English form of Gaspar, traditionally one of the three kings whom medieval legend transformed into the 'wise man' who arrived at Bethlehem to worship the infant Jesus. The name was found in England in the fourteenth century, and spread to Scotland, where it has been used sparingly as Jasper, Jaspar and Jesper. Jasper Cumming, clerk to the diocese of Moray, was a commissioner to Parliament for Inverness in 1587.

JEAN (f) O.Fr. *Jehane* Latinised *Johanna*, but in Scotland many women named JANE are called Jean. Variants are Jean, Jeane, JEANNE, Jeanie, Jeanine and Jeanetta. Jean has always been a popular name in Scotland. John, Duke of Albany, had a natural daughter by Jean Abernethy, called Eleonora, and she married in 1547, John de l' Hôpital, Comte de Choisy, at Fountainbleau. King James V had a natural daughter Jean, by Elizabeth Bethune. 'Jean or Joan', daughter of Robert Arbuthnott of that Ilk, married James Clephane of Hilcairney *c.* 1557. Jean Armour (1767–1834) was the faithful wife of the poet Burns, and inspired more than a dozen songs, of which 'Of a' the airts the wind can blaw' is probably the best. The 'blue-eyed lassie' of his song, 'I gaed a waeful gate yestreen', was Jean Jeffrey (1773–1850).

JEANNE (f) Derived from Jean, and often rendered Jeanie or Jeannie. In Scott's novel *The Heart of Midlothian*, Jeanie Deans, douce Davie's daughter, is a 'docile, quiet, gentle, and even timid country maiden'. The prototype of Jeanie was Helen Walker, to whom the great novelist erected a memorial in Irongray churchyard. Jeannie Robertson (1908–75), a notable ballad singer, came from the ranks of the travelling folk.

JEMIMA (f) Heb. meaning 'dove'. The biblical Jemima was the oldest of the three daughters born to Job, a man of substance in the land of Uz. Jemima and her sisters Kezia and Keren-happuch, were, with their seven brothers, co-heirs (OT, Job 42:13–15). In 'all the land were no women so fair as the daughters of Job'. The name was favoured by the Puritans in the seventeenth century, and it has been suggested that it may have occasionally been used as a feminine form of JAMES. Jemmina, Jemimah, and Jemina, possibly also Jemma, are variant spellings, and Mima is a pet name. King Charles II had a natural daughter in 1650, by Lady Shannon, named Charlotte Jemima Henrietta Maria. Jemima Falconer, wife of Sir Philip Forester, appears in Scott's novel, *My Aunt Margaret's Mirror* (1827).

JENNA (f) A Latinised form of JENNIE or JENNY, and currently popular.

JENNIE, JENNY (f) Usually diminutive of JANET and JENNIFER, and occasionally for JANE. Jenny Geddes was a High Street greengrocer who is said to have hurled a stool at the Bishop of Edinburgh who was attempting to introduce the *Book of Common Prayer* in St Giles' Cathedral in 1637, but there is no contempory evidence to support the story. The poet Burns gave the name Jenny Geddes to the mare he rode on his Border tour. At the time of his unconsummated affair in Edinburgh with Clarinda (Mrs McLehose), the bard liaised with Jenny Clow who bore him a son, and died in 1791 in poor circumstances. Jenny Cairns, a creditor of Ellangowan, appears in Scott's novel *Guy Mannering*. Jenna is a pet name.

JENNIFER (f) Welsh *Gwenhwyfar*, 'fair and yielding'. The name was that of the legendary King Arthur's wife, Guinevere, and became Jennifer through the Cornish tongue. According to Dr G.F. Black, Guinevere gave rise to the surnames Wanders and Wannour. Noel Coward (1899–1973) named a character Jennifer in *The Young Idea* (1923), and this gave impetus to use of the name, along with the popular film actress, Jennifer Jones. Short forms of the name are JENNY, JENNIE, and Jenn, all shared with JANET.

JEROME (m) Gr. *Ieronumos*, Latinised *Hieronymus*. It was the name of a king of Syracuse, a grandson of a Rhodian philosopher, also of Hieronymus Sophronius (340–420), better known as St Jerome, who made a Latin translation of the Bible, which was the basis of *The Vulgate*. Hieronymus or Jerome Lindsay (1562–

1642) of Annatland, was Lord Lyon King of Arms, 1621–30. Its revival in modern times is probably due to the composer, Jerome Kern (1885–1945). Surnames derived from the name are Jerome itself, Jerram, Jerrems, Jarram and Jeromeson.

JESSICA (f) Heb 'He [ie God] beholds'. The name appears in the bible as Iscah (OT, Genesis ll:29). Its use in Britain is almost certainly due to the influence of Shakespeare's play, *The Merchant of Venice*, in which Shylock's daughter is named Jessica. For a time the name was considered Jewish. It is within the top hundred girls' names in Scotland, and gained in popularity due probably to the actress Jessica Lange. Diminutives are Jess and Jesse (a male name in its own right). See also JANET.

JESSIE (f) In Scotland is usually a pet form of JANET, and his its own variants, usually Jessie and Jessy. See also JANET. Jessie M. King (1875–1949), daughter of a minister of New Kilpatrick, was a talented artist.

JILL *See* GILLIAN.

JOAN (m, f) Always represented as a contraction of the Latin JOHANNA, and has been applied to men. Joan, son of Connal, 'a wicked man', scorned St Columba in the sixth century, and was drowned in a storm. In the Middle Ages the name was used extensively. Joan, sister of Edward III of England, married David II, King of Scots (1329–71). Joan, niece of Cardinal Beaufort, married James I of Scotland, *c.* 1424. Occasionally Joan is synonymous with JEAN. In spite of the film *Joan of Arc*, which starred the late Ingrid Bergman, and the fact that several other actresses have borne the name Joan, it has declined in popularity.

JOANNA, JOANNE (f) Feminine form of Johannes (JOHN), and much used in the nineteenth century. The name has been well used in Scotland. Joanna, widow of Sir Thomas Murray of Bothwell, married *c.* 1362, Sir Archibald Douglas, 'the Grim', a natural son of 'the good' Sir James Douglas. The name remained in use and both spellings have overtaken JOAN, with Joanne, the French form, being now highly favoured.

JOCELYN (m, f) O.G. *Gautelen,* but the meaning is obscure: possibly from some old tribal name. The name was first used as masculine, and is of considerable antiquity. Jocelyn, Abbot of Melrose, was consecrated Bishop of Glasgow in 1175, and died in 1199. Use as a girls' name is comparatively modern and not widespread. Variant spellings are Jocelin, Joceline, Joscelyn, Josiline and Josslyn. Josie is a pet name.

JOCK (m) A popular pet name for JOHN, with JACK as an alternative. A 'Jock' is the name given to a Highland soldier.

JODIE (f) A variant of Judy, diminutive of JUDITH.

JOHANNA (f) This was the usual Latin form of JOAN (*see also* JOANNA) but appears in the scriptures in the genealogy of JOSEPH as masculine (NT, Luke 3:27), and again (24:10) as one of the women who ministered to Jesus. After the Reformation, it came to be used as a feminine name and, with the variant Johanne, is in current use.

JOHN (m) Heb. *Johanan*, meaning 'God has been gracious'. The usual Latin form is Joannes and in Gaelic is IAIN. The name goes back to biblical times. John the Baptist was the son of Zacharius and ELIZABETH (cousin of the virgin MARY), and at circumcision his name was changed from Zacharius. The existence of the apostle John can be queried as there is evidence that the gospel attributed to him was written by later theologians. John was a prolific name in the time of the Roman Empire and the name of seven popes. John of Tinmouth wrote a life of St Columba, compiled mainly from Adamnan, 697–704. John Balliol, King of Scots, 1292–1302, was of Anglo-Flemish extraction. The name has continued to be popular down through the ages. John Broadwood (1732–1812), born at Oldhamstocks, was a maker of musical instruments. John Muir (1838–1914) from Dunbar emigrated to the USA and became a famous conservationist. The novelist John Buchan (1875–1940) was Governor-General of Canada, 1935–40. John Grierson (1898–1972), born in Kilmarnock, has been dubbed 'The Father of Documentary Films'. Many surnames are derived from John, including Johnson, Jones, Johnman, Jackson, Hancock and Hankin. 'John Barleycorn' is malt liquor personified. The name was used by Burns as a pseudonym in his 'Address of the Scottish Distillers to the Right Honourable William Pitt', which was printed in the *Gazetteer* and the *New Daily Advertiser*. He also wrote 'John Barleycorn – A Ballad', praising whisky. Sir Walter Scott used the name frequently in his novels. The name is within the top ten most popular boys' names in Scotland. Diminutives are JOCK and JACK.

JONATHAN (m) Heb. 'Jehovah's gift'. In the scriptures there are three Jonathans; the son of Saul, the priest's son who served DAVID, and Jonathan Maccabaeus. Saul's eldest son Jonathan was a devoted friend of DAVID, whose side he took when Saul turned against him. He was killed fighting the Philistines (OT, 1 Chronicles 10:2), and David's lament bears the oft-quoted words, 'How are the mighty fallen'. Literary allusions to David and Jonathan, as the symbol of enduring friendship, were at one period common. The name was quietly used in the Middle Ages. Jonathan, Bishop of Dunblane, is recorded in 1198. At the siege of Boston in 1776, the British applied the name 'Brother Jonathan' to any American. The nickname may have contributed to a decline in use, but since the Second World War the name has been favoured and is now within the top thirty boys' names. There is some confusion with John, and Jonathan is sometimes found as a variant of John. Other spellings are Jonathen, Johnothon and Jonothan. The diminutive Jon is occasionally used independently.

JORDAN (m, f) Heb. *Hardan*, 'to descend', and because of the River Jordan, usually interpreted as 'flowing down'. The name was brought to Britain by returning crusaders, who also carried home Jordan water for baptisms. The name is occasionally feminine. Jordano de Riddel, the younger son of Sir Arketille de Riddel, witnessed several charters of William the Lion between 1165 and 1171. Jordan has given rise to the surnames Jordan, Jordans, and Jordanson.

JOSEPH (m) Heb. meaning 'Jehovah adds [children]'. Men of this name mentioned in the scriptures are Jacob's elder son by RACHEL (OT, Genesis 35:24), his favourite, to whom he gave the coat of many colours; Joseph, son of Heli, husband of the virgin Mary (NT, Matthew 1:18), and the patron saint of carpenters; Joseph of Arimathea (NT, Matthew 27:57), and Joseph Justus, called Barsabas (NT, Acts 1:23). During the Middle Ages the name was in constant use, but not prolific. There was no revival of interest in the name after the Reformation, but it came more into use in the eighteenth century. Joseph Hume of Ninewells was father of David Hume (1711–76), the historian. Joseph Williamson (1706–95), advocate, was a son of 'Dainty Davie' Williamson, the seven-times-married minister of the West Kirk of Edinburgh. The Gaelic rendering is *Ioseph*. Joe is a short form and Josephine is feminine.

JOSEPHINE (f) Fr. diminutive of Josephe, feminine form of JOSEPH. Marie Rose Josephine (1763–1814) married (as her second husband) Napoleon Bonaparte. She was divorced from him in 1809, but retained the title of Empress. The Gaelic form is *Seosaidh*. Variants are Josepha, Josephe and Josette. Josie is a pet name, but is sometimes a forename independently.

JOSHUA (m) Heb. 'Jehova is generous'. In the bible, Joshua, son of Nun, is second only to Moses in the story of the Israelites' trek into the promised land. He led the second generation across the Jordan and divided the land between the twelve tribes of Israel and the Levites. Joshua received the city of Timnathserah, where he died

(OT, Deuteronomy 31:7). The name came into use in Scotland after the Reformation, but until recently was used sparingly. Joshua Sheshan, gunsmith, was admitted a burgess of Edinburgh in 1662, and Josh Grant was a clockmaker in Calton, Glasgow, 1830. Scott has Joshua Geddes as a Quaker in *Redgauntlet*. The usual short form is Josh.

JOSIAH (m) Heb. 'Jehovah heals [the mother at the time of birth]'. The name has never been common in Scotland. Josias Stewart, son of Andrew, Master of Ochiltree, is on record in 1587. The best-known man with this Christian name was Josiah Wedgewood (1730–95), the Staffordshire potter.

JOYCE (m, f) An old personal name, probably of Celtic origin. It has been said to come from the Latin word for joy, but this, and the idea that it is a feminine form of Jocelyn, is doubtful. It was the name of a seventh-century Breton prince and saint, Latinised Judocius. In the Middle Agnes, when it was used more as a masculine name, it often had the form Josse or Joisse. It came to be more commonly used as a girls' name. Joyce, daughter of Sir Edward Aston, whose son became Baron Forfar in 1627, had a daughter Joyce, who married Sir Martin Culpepper of Deane, Oxfordshire. Joyce also became a surname. James Joyce (1882–1941), the Dublin-born writer and vocalist, kept the name before the public. As a forename it is in regular but quiet use.

JUDITH (f) Heb., *Yehudith*, 'Jewess'. A biblical name with historic associations. Judith, daughter of Berri the Hittite and Bashemath, married Esau, brother of Jacob

(OT, Genesis 26:34). Judith, daughter of Charles the Bald of France, married Baldwin I, grandson of Lideric, who founded Flanders in 792. In 856 as a child-bride, she married Aethelwulf, King of Wessex, who died in 858. She passed effortless into the arms of her stepson, Ethelbald, who died in 860. By her marriage to Baldwin, she had two sons, Baldwin II and Rudolph of Cambrai. Adele, sister of William the Conqueror, was mother of Judith, who married Waltheof of Northumbria; and their daughter Maud or Matilda, married David I, King of Scots. The name was uncommon before the seventeenth century, and since then has been in regular, but not wide use. Judith, wife of Stephen 'Bible' Butler, appears in Scott's *Heart of Midlothian*. The diminutives Jodi, Jodie, Jody and Judy, have all been used independently, especially Jodie. The name was Latinised *Juditha*, and the Gaelic form is SIOBHAN. In Ireland Judith and Julia are often interchangeable.

JULIA, JULIE (f) Lat., the feminine form of JULIUS, and appears in both spellings, Julie, the French form being the most popular, and occasionally linked with Ann or Anne, from which comes Juliana. The popularity of Julie may be due to the influence of the actresses Julie Andrews (born Julie Wells) and Julie Harris. Juliet, another form, interesting because of Shakespeare's *Romeo and Juliet*, is uncommon in Scotland. In some cases in Scotland the name Julia or Julie, derives from GILES (see also EGIDIA). Juliana, daughter of COSPATRIC of Dunbar, who died before 1139, married Randulph de Merlay, Lord of Morpeth. Juliana or

Egidia, daughter of Sir Duncan Campbell of Glenorchy, married John Gordon, heir apparent of Buckie in 1626. Juliana, daughter of Sir David Home of Wedderburn, killed in 1524, had a daughter Juliana, who married Sir John Gordon of Lochinvar.

JULIAN *See* JULIUS.

JULIUS (m) Lat., 'bearded'. The name of a Roman *gens*, from which sprang Caius Julius Caesar (100–44 BC), who had a daughter Julia, who married Pompey. The Romans supposed the name Julius was derived from the Greek word meaning 'downy'. Pope Julius I was in power, AD 337–52. The name came to Britain with Cesare Aelmare (1558–1636), physician to Queen Elizabeth, who dropped his patronymic and adopted the Christian name of Julius. The name was never prolific in Scotland, but sometimes appears as JULIAN, which is in current use, and can be male or female. The feminine form is usually JULIA or JULIE.

JUNE (f) This is simply the name of the sixth month of the year. Juno was the 'venerable ox-eyed' wife of Jupiter, and in Roman mythology the 'Queen of Heaven'. The month, however, was not named after her, but from the *junio res* or soldiers of the state. Its use as a name appears to date from the First World War, and although in current use it has declined in popularity in recent years.

K

KAREN (f) A Danish diminutive of Katarina, which has been used since the 1930s. It is now in high favour, within the top twenty girls' names. Variants are Karan, Karin, Karon, Karyn, Caron, Caronne, Carren and Caryn.

KATHARINE, KATHERINE (f) Gr. *Katharos*, 'pure'. The name, synonymous with CATHARINE / CATHERINE, is of some antiquity, and was brought to Scotland by returning crusaders, mindful of the legend of St Katherine of Alexandria, who was put to death after confessing the gospel at a sacrificial feast, AD 307. The name was Latinised Katerina in early records. Katerina de Creichton and her husband, Alexander Seytoun of Perbrothe, had a charter of half of the lands of Leuchlande in the Lordship of Brechin, 1472–3. The name became very popular in Scotland and is still within the top fifty girls' names registered annually. KATHRYN is a variant and the Gaelic rendering is CATRIONA. Short forms are Kate, Katie, Katy and Kathy.

KATHLEEN (f) The English form of the Irish CAITLIN. The popular song (American, not Irish) 'I'll take you home again Kathleen', first heard in the 1870s, undoubtedly gave the name approval. Cathleen was one of Flora McIvor's maids in Scott's *Waverley*. Kitty and Kay are short forms.

KATHRYN *See* KATHERINE

KAY (m, f) The name appeared anciently, and may be derived from the Latin name *Caius*, borrowed by the Celts, and in Welsh rendered *Kei*, said to mean 'fiery' and/or 'rejoicer'. In Arthurian legend Kay is one of the more famous knights of the round table. Kay became a surname, but in modern times also appears as a diminutive of KATHLEEN, sometimes spelt Kaye. Probably the actress Kay Kendall (Justine McCarthy, 1926–59), helped make the name popular and influenced its use as an independent name.

KAYLEIGH, KAYLEY (f) This name may be a form of Kylie, derived from the Australian boomerang; curled stick. However, Kylie was until recently almost entirely confined to Australia, and its current use in Scotland may be due to that country's actress-singer, Kylie Minogue. It seems possible that Kayleigh and Kayley may simply be adapted from KAY, by analogy with KELLY, used both as a forename and surname.

KEIR (m) This is a surname of territorial origin from lands in Stirlingshire, and recorded in the thirteenth century. However, a secondary origin is from *Ciar*, a personal name derived from 'dusky' or swarthy' (see CIARAN). It is now found as a forename (twenty were registered in 1990) and surname. Probably the best-known bearer of the name was the pioneer Labour politician, James Keir Hardie (1856–1915), but his real name was Kerr. He was a natural son of Mary Kerr, a farm 'outbye' worker at Legbrannoch in Bothwell parish, and William Aitken, a miner, identified as the father at Hamilton Sheriff Court. She married David Hardie, a joiner, in 1859.

KEIRA (f) Feminine form of Keiran (see CIARAN).

KEITH (m) A territorial surname, it is now within the top one hundred boys' Christian names registered annually. Keith is an East Lothian place name. Malcolm de Keth witnessed a gift to the Abbey of Kelso, c. 1190. Bernard de Keth was a juror on an inquest at Berwick in 1296. It appears as a full-blown surname when Andrew Kethe of Enyrrugy was one of the hostages for King James I in 1425. The family became entrenched in the North-east, and before 1431 Sir William Keith was made a Lord of Parliament. The Keiths were Marischals of Scotland, but the 10th Earl was forfeited for his part in the Jacobite Rising of 1715.

KELLY (m, f) Although usually thought of as an Irish surname, the name is also Scottish, and probably derived from the lands of Kelly near Arbroath in Angus. John de Kelly was Abbot of Arbroath in 1373. Waulter of Kylle had a safe conduct to England in 1424, and James Kelle was a Notary Public in the diocese of St Andrews in 1526. The name was common in East Lothian and Berwickshire in the sixteenth and seventeenth centuries. MacKelly is an old Galloway surname, but possibly derives from *MacCeallach*, 'son of Celach', and may have been imported from Ireland. It has come into favour as a forename for males and more often for females (see also KAYLEIGH). Kellie and Kelley are variants and Kel or Kell are pet names.

KENNETH (m) Gael. *Coinneach*, 'comely' or 'handsome',

and considered to derive from *cin-aedha*, 'firesprung'. The two names are now synonymous. St Cainnech (517–600), an Irish Abbot, visited St Columba at Iona. Kenneth MacAlpin united the Scottish and Pictish nations in 844, and re-established the Columban church at Dunkeld. Two other kings bore the name: Kenneth, son of Malcolm, reigned 971–95, and Kenneth, son of Dubh, reigned 997–1004. *Coinneach*, progenitor of the Mackenzie chiefs, descended from Colin of the Aird, and the name has always been favoured by the clan. It is also used nowadays in England by families with no Scottish background. Pet names are Ken and Kenny.

KERRY (m, f) The name is derived mainly from the Irish county, originally the abode of 'Ciar's people'. It was used as a male name in Australia during the Second World War, but here is now considered solely as a girl's name, stemming possibly from Carrie. Kerry is now within the top fifty girls' names registered yearly in Scotland. Variants are Keri, Kerri, Kerie and Keree. Sometimes the name is hyphenated with Anne.

KEVIN (m) Irish Gael. *Caomhin*, 'born handsome', but in some cases may be a variant of Cavens, a surname derived from the lands of that name in Kirkbean parish, Kirkcudbrightshire. Gilbert de Cavens was presented to the church of Kirkinner in 1402. John Kevan, tenant in Barbershall, Parton, is on record in 1792. Testaments exist for five Kevands in the Wigtown Commissariot in the eighteenth century. Kevin is now within the top thirty boys' names registered annually.

KIERAN, KIERON (m) Irish Gael. *Ciaran*, 'dusky', or

'dark'. It has in fact the same meaning as CIARAN, but evolved independently. An early reference to the name is Cearthann or Keiran grandson of Mughdhorn (from whom the Mountains of Mourne derive the name), son of Colla Uais, living around 332. It was the name of several saints, two more distinguished than the others: St Ciaran of Clonmacnoise, and St Ciaran of Ossory, who became a bishop about 538. The actor Kieron Moore (Kieron O'Hanrahan) has given the name publicity since the 1940s. Keira and Kiera have been recorded as feminine forms.

KIM (m, f) Pet name derived from KIMBERLEY, and now used more than the parent name. Kim (Kimball O'Hara) was the young hero of Rudyard Kipling's famous novel of the name, published in 1901, and this may have influenced some parents to give boys the name. The name went into decline but re-emerged in the late 1920s as a feminine name and is now within the top one hundred names. The impetus may have come from a female character in Eda Ferber's *Showboat* (1926), filmed three times. The actress Kim Novak (Marilyn Novak, born Chicago 1933) may have influenced the use.

KIMBERLEY (m, f) The name is derived from the diamond-mining town of the name in South Africa, named after Lord Kimberley, who in turn bore a name which originated in an English place name. It had publicity during the Boer War, and many soldiers returning home named sons Kimberley. The name was used sparingly until the late 1940s, when it rallied as a feminine name. Variants are Kimberleigh, Kimberley, Kimberli and Kimberly. The pet name KIM is now more popular in Scotland.

KIRSTEN (f) The forename Kirsten has been in use in Scotland longer than in any other part of the United Kingdom. In many cases it is a Scandinavian form of Christine, a form of CHRISTIAN. Kirsty, Kersteen, Kirstine and Kirstyn are variant forms.

KRISTOPHER (m) A form of CHRISTOPHER now becoming popular in Scotland, and probably influenced by the American actor/folk-singer, Kris Kristofferson.

KYLE (m) An Ayrshire district name which appears as a surname early in the fifteenth century. Walter of Kyle had safe conduct into England in 1424. Donald Kyle was admitted a burgess of Edinburgh in 1517, and the testament of William Kyle, Burgess of Glasgow, was confirmed in 1578. The name possibly derives from Coel Hen, a ruler of the district of Kyle around AD 400, probably also the original 'Old King Cole'. The Kyles of Laurel Hill, Co. Derry, Ireland were of Scottish descent. The name has come into use as a forename, perhaps with some Irish influence, and is now within the top seventy boys' names. It may have influenced some other feminine names such as KELLY and KYLIE.

KYLIE (f) In some cases the name is possibly a feminine form of KYLE, but its recent rise to popularity is due to Australian actress/singer Kylie Minogue. See also KAYLEIGH.

L

LACHLAN (m) There are two possible derivations for this name. One, according to Alexander Bain, is from the Scandinavian *Lochlann* or Lake-land (Fjord-land perhaps). The other possibility is that it is of Irish origin, with a similar meaning – *lough-lann*, 'loch habitation'. In Irish records Lochlain MacLochlain appears in the twelfth century. The Scottish clan MacLachlan descend from Lachlan, son of Gilpatrick, who witnessed a charter to the Abbey of Paisley, c. 1238. He may have descended from Niall of the Nine Hostages, who reigned in Ireland around AD 400. Richard, son of Lachlan, is mentioned as a custumer of Stirling, c. 1327. Lachlan MacLachlan of that Ilk had a safe conduct to France in 1536. The name has been well used by families in the West Highlands and in the Hebrides, but is now outwith the top one hundred boys' names. In Gaelic it is rendered *Lachlann*. Short forms are Lachie, Lachy, Lackie, Lack, and Lacky.

LAURA (f) Lat., but of obscure origin. Lauricia, Laurina and Laurencia, are feminine forms of LAWRENCE in Roman times and Lora appears in England in the fourteenth century. Laura appears in England in the fifteenth century and may be derived from that name, or was originally a pet name for Laurencia. The name was immortalised by Petrarch, the Italian poet, who addressed sonnets to a lady named Laura, possibly

Laura de Noves. For a long period it was not as popular as LORA, but is now a fashionable forename. Variants are Lauri, Lauretta, Laurette, Loretta and occasionally LORRAINE.

LAUREN (f) This either a variant of LAURA or a modern feminine form of LAWRENCE. It has made an astonishing leap to become one of the most favoured names in Scotland. Perhaps it is due to the repeat showings on TV of films starring Lauren Bacall (Betty Joan Perske), widow of the late Humphrey Bogart. Loren is a variant.

LAURENCE, LAWRENCE (m) Derived from the Latin name *Laurentius*, through the French Laurence, and stemming from the maritime city of Laurentium, south of Rome. The place-name derives from the laurels which grew there in abundance. Laurel was used to decorate persons of distinction, and the term 'Poet Laureate' is used in this sense. St Laurentius the Deacon was martyred in the third century under Valerian, by being roasted on a grid-iron. The old parish church of Edzell, in Angus, was dedicated to St Laurence. Laurence, a Dominican, was elected bishop of Argyll *c.* 1263, and Laurentius was archdeacon of Brechin in 1368. The name has been used both as forename and surname. John Lourens was admitted a burgess of Aberdeen in 1541, and John Lourance was a notary at Duns in 1663. Other surnames derived from Laurence are Laurie, Larkins, Law, and in some cases Lowry. In Gaelic the name is rendered *Labhruinn*. The eponymous ancestor of the MacLaren chiefs was Labhran, an abbot of the old Celtic church, who held the lands of Auchtow in western Strathearn, and the plant badge of the clan is the laurel. In Scott's novel, *The Pirate*, Lawrence Linkletter is the old cousin who left Halcro, 'the wee bit island'. Laurence Scoley also appears in the novel as a servant of Magnus Triol and his daughters. Laurence Macdonald (1798–1878), born at Gask in Perthshire, was a famous sculptor.

LAVINIA (f) The etymology is nebulous, but the Lavinia of classical literature, daughter of King Latinius, in Greek legend, may have been given her name from the town of Lavinium, originally Latium. Lavinia was a popular name during the Renaissance, but faded. Its revival in Scotland is due to James Thomson (1700–48), the poet of *The Seasons*, the biblical story of Boaz and Ruth under the names Palemon and Lavinia. Lavinia Derwent, born on a Border farm began writing for 'Children's Hour' and wrote a number of books, popular in the 1970s, including cameos of her childhood life.

LEAH (f) Heb., 'tender eyed'. The biblical Leah was the elder daughter of Laban, son of Nahor, and sister of RACHEL. They both became wives of Jacob, and Leah bore him six sons and a daughter DINAH (OT, Genesis 30:21). The name was introduced to England by the Puritans in the late sixteenth century. It was fairly well used in the nineteenth century, but faded in the 1920s, only to recover in the 1970s. It is in regular use in Scotland, but outwith the top one hundred girls' names. Lea is a diminutive form, frequently linked with ANN.

LEANNE (f) A modern name combining Lea and ANNE and often written Lea-Anne. Lianne is a variant. While Lee is occasionally used as a diminutive, the name evolved differently.

LEE (m, f) Early references point to Lee being an English surname, perhaps derived from *Leah*, 'meadow', but sometimes given the meaning 'gentle being'. The name appeared in Scotland in 1246 when Alan de Leya witnessed a charter by Alexander, son of Walter the Steward. Phelippe de la Leye swore fealty in 1296. The use of Lee as a forename is fairly modern and not confined to men. American film star Lee Marvin probably influenced its use, and the variant Leigh has also been used both as a forename and a surname for men and women. The actress Vivien Leigh (Vivien Hartley, 1913–67) starred with Clark Gable (1901–60) in Margaret Mitchell's famous blockbuster, *Gone with the Wind*. Occasionally Lee is a pet name for Ashley and/or Ashleigh, but is different in origin from LEAH. Other variant forms are Ley, Lay, Laye, Lye, and Lyes. In Gaelic-speaking parts of Scotland Lees derives from *MacIlliosa (Mac gill' Iosa)*, 'son of the servant of Jesus'. It is a common surname on Deeside. Scott has characters called Lee in *Kenilworth, Woodstock* and *The Talisman*. As with Lea, Lee is sometimes linked with Ann, Anna and/or Anne.

LENA (f) A short form of MAGDALENE, in recent times associated with the vocalist Lena Horne, born in New York, 1917, who appeared in numerous films.

LEONORA *See* ELEANOR.

LESLEY (f) Feminine spelling of LESLIE. Lesley (died 1843), daughter of Robert Baillie of Mayfield, Ayrshire, attracted the poet Burns, and inspired 'Saw ye Bonie Lesley', 1792, and 'Blythe hae I been on you hill', 1793.

LESLIE (m) A well-known surname derived from the lands of *Lesslyn*, now Leslie, in Aberdeenshire. The progenitor of the Leslies was Bartolph the Fleming, who came to Scotland from Flanders about 1057. The name has been used as a male Christian name from 1832 at least. LESLEY is the feminine form, and Les is a pet name.

LEWIS (m) O.G., *Chlodowig*, 'famous warrior', Latinised as *Ludovicus*. The French rendered the name LOUIS, and it was the name of a line of eighteen kings. The name was brought to England by the Normans and soon found its way to Scotland, where frequently it became LUDOVIC. The Gaelic form is *Luthais*. Lewis Innes (1651–1738) was the older brother of Father Thomas Innes, the historian. The name was popular in several branches of the GORDON family. Lewis Grassic Gibbon was the pen-name of J. Leslie Mitchell (1901–35), author of *A Scots Quair* and other novels. The name is in regular use, and is just within the top forty boys' names registered annually in Scotland.

LIAM (m) An Irish form of William which has, like RYAN, had a remarkable rise to popularity and is within the top thirty boys' names. It will probably retain if not gain in status, as a result of Irish/American actor Liam Neeson being the hero in the film *Rob Roy*.

LILIAS, LILLIAS (f) Derived from *Liliana*, the Italian form of LILY, and much favoured for centuries in Scotland.

The surname Lillie does not appear to be associated, and probably that name is territorial; from lands named Lillock, in the barony of Ballinbreich, Fife. John [Graham], 3rd Earl of Montrose, had a daughter Lilias, who married *c.* 1586, John, Lord Fleming. Lilias, born 1621, daughter of Sir David Lindsay of Balcarres, died young in 1632. Variants include Lilie, Lilium, Lilley, Lillia and Lillean.

LILY (f) Generally a flower name, but in some cases derived from ELIZABETH or from LILIAS. There is a tradition that the lily sprang from the repentant tears of EVE, as she went forth from Paradise. In Christian art the lily is represented as an emblem of chastity, innocence and purity, hence the sayings 'As pure as a lily' and 'lily white'. Also, in the popular hymn, 'By cool Siloam's shady rill', the second line is 'How sweet the lily grows'. A song, once popular, was 'Lily of Laguna'. The name was well-favoured in Scotland, even in Gaelic-speaking areas, but has lost ground. Lily Cameron (1791–1875) from Stornoway parish, Lewis, emigrated with her husband Duncan 'Seoldair' Morrison, to Compton County, Quebec, Canada, in 1852. Lil is a pet name.

LLOYD (m) Welsh *llwyd*, 'grey, holy'. This common surname and forename has spread to every English-speaking country. It was of course highlighted by David Lloyd George (1863–1945), Prime Minister, 1916–22, who was raised to the peerage. It has been sparingly used in Scotland.

LINDA (f) O.G., from *linde*, 'serpent', a symbol of wisdom. It is often considered as a pet form of BELINDA,

Malenda, Melinda and Rosalinda, all of which can be used independently.

LINDSAY (m, f) Appears as a surname in Scotland as early as the twelfth century and is territorial, probably from a place-name in Normandy or Flanders. It has been much used as a Christian name for boys and girls since the 1930s, but currently is applied more to girls. Variants are Lindsay, Lindsey, Linsay, Linsey, Linzi, Linzie, Lyndsay, Lyndsey, Lynsay and Lyndsey. Lin and Lyn are pet names.

LISA (f) A popular variant of ELIZABETH.

LORA, LORI (f) Variants of LAURA, not prolific in Scotland, but in current use.

LORNA (f) The name was created by R.D. Blackmore (1825–1900) for the heroine of his novel *Lorna Doone* (1869). It is derived from the place-name Lorn or Lorne, ancestral home of the MacDougalls. Lorna becomes Lady Lorna Dugal. The name is still in use, but just outwith the top one hundred girls' names registered annually in Scotland.

LORRAINE (f) O.Fr., derived in most cases from the province of Lorraine, but appears occasionally as a variant of LAURA. In the thirteenth century it occurs as a surname, and there are still people of this name in Scotland. Roger Loraine witnessed an agreement between the Chapter of Moray and Sir Alan Durward in 1233. The mother of Mary, Queen of Scots, born at Linlithgow in 1542, was Mary of Lorraine. As a forename it spread from France to Scotland, and it is still in regular use.

LOUIS (m) The French form of LEWIS. The much-loved literary man, Robert Louis Stevenson (1850–94), was baptised Robert Lewis, the name coming from his maternal grandfather, the Rev. Lewis Balfour (1777–1860), minister of Colinton parish, but his middle name was changed to Louis because of his father's aversion to an Edinburgh councillor named Lewis. See also LUDOVIC.

LOUISA, LOUISE (f) Respectively the Latin and French forms of LOUIS. Louisa was long the most popular rendering in Scotland, but the modern favourite is Louise. The testament of Dame Louisa Aitchison, widow of Sir John Rochead, Baronet of Inverleith, was confirmed at Edinburgh in 1750. Louisa Murray (1745–1840), a younger daughter of Lionel, Earl of Dysart, became Countess in her own right in 1821. Pet forms include Louie, Lulu, Lula, Lulie and even Loosy, the name given to Princess Louise, fourth daughter of Queen Victoria, who married John George [Campbell], 9th Duke of Argyll, in 1871. The Gaelic form of the name is *Liùsaidh*.

LUCAS (m) Lat., from the personal name *Lucius*, a form of Luke. Lucas appears as a surname at Westow, Suffolk, towards the end of the twelfth century, and in Berwickshire, Scotland, by the fifteenth century. A family named Luke appear to have owned the estate of Claythorn in Lanarkshire before 1589. Capt. Richard Lucas, of General Wade's Regiment, was admitted a burgess of Glasgow in 1724. Some people who bore the surname MacLucas were said to form a sept of Clan

Lamont, and they anglicised the name as Luke. As a forename Luke is in current, but not wide, use.

LUCINDA *See* LUCY.

LUCIUS (m) The name LUCAS stemmed from *Lucius*, a Latin praenomen, possibly derived from *lux*, 'light', and appears in this form. St Lucius was Bishop of Rome, 253–4, and there were two later popes of that name. Lucius emerged as an ordinary forename after the Renaissance. Occasionally Lucia is found. Lucius Cary (1610–43), of English birth, held the Scottish title of (2nd) Viscount Falkland. He was killed at Newbury. The 3rd, 6th and 7th, 10th, 13th and 14th viscounts were all named Lucius, and the 15th is Lucius Edward Plantagenet, the premier Viscount of Scotland.

LUCRETIA, LUCRECE (f) Lat. feminine form of *Lucretius*, the name of a Roman *gens*. Lucretia, said to mean 'riches', wife of Collantius, was raped by Tarquin, and her subsequent suicide caused the expulsion of the Tarquins from Rome. The Italian Lucrezia di Borgia, said to have been a daughter of Pope Alexander VI (consecrated 1492), was three times wed, and had a natural son, Genaro. The name has never been common in Scotland. Lucrece, natural daughter of John, 5th Lord Fleming, married about 1593, Robert Graham of the Fauld, in England. Lucretiae, daughter of David Spens of Wormiston, married Patrick Forbes of Corse, consecrated Bishop of Aberdeen in 1618. The Gaelic form of the name is *Lucreis*.

LUCY (f) Lat. 'light', and the feminine form of LUCIUS, while Lucilla was a diminutive. Anciently it signified a child born at dawn, and the goddess Lucina was reckoned the patroness of childbirth. St Lucy was a Sicilian martyr much loved in the Middle Ages, and patroness of those with eye afflictions. The name appears occasionally as Lucette, Lucia, Lucinda, Lucilla and Lucille. Lucy Douglas, daughter of William, 11th Earl of Angus, married Robert, Lord Maxwell, in 1669. Lucia, a younger daughter of Sir George Hamilton of Dunalong, fourth son of James, 1st Earl of Abercorn, married Donogh O'Brien of Lemineagh. Lucy Ashton is the gentle daughter of Sir William Ashton, in Scott's novel, *The Bride of Lammermoor*. In his novel, *Waverley*, Lucy St Aubin is 'a beautiful and wealthy' maid.

LUDOVIC, LUDOVICK (m) Derived from *Ludovicus*, the Latin form of LEWIS and became popular in Scotland in the seventeenth century. Ludovic Lindsay succeeded to the title of 16th Earl of Crawford in 1639. Sir Ludovick Gordon, 2nd Bart of Gordonstoun, had a charter under the Great Seal, in 1649, confirming to him the lands and baronies of Achry, Dollas and others. In 1689 Col Ludovick Grant of that Ilk, raised a regiment of foot for King William. Ludovick Houston (1672–1727) of Johnstone, Renfrewshire, married Agnes Walkinshaw, a relative of Clementina Walkinshaw, who figures in Neil Munro's story, *The Red Shoes*. Sir Ludovic Kennedy, the veteran author and broadcaster, whose wife is the former ballerina, Moira Shearer, star of the film, *The Red Shoes*, is descended from the 11th Earl of Cassillis. The Gaelic form of Ludovic is *Maoldònaich*. Ludo is a pet name.

LUKE (m) *See* LUCAS. The biblical Luke, physician, evangelist and saint, was probably born in Antioch and is thought to have died in Greece. He was the author of the third gospel, written *c.* AD 80, and its continuation, the Acts of the Apostles. The name came to Britain as Lucas, but more families adopted the shorter form of Luke. It is both a forename and a surname. John Luke was a baillie of Rutherglen in 1564, and the Lukes of Claythorn, were a well-known Lanarkshire family. Luke also evolved as an English form of *Mac Gille Moluag*, 'son of the servant of Moluag', who was a contempory of St Columba. The Gaelic form is now *Lucais*.

LYDIA (F) Gr., 'woman of Lydia'. Lydia of Thyatira is mentioned in the scriptures (NT, Acts 16:14–15), and in apocryphal writings is identified as a daughter of Joseph of Nazareth. The name came to Britain in the seventeenth century, and is currently in use in Scotland. In Jane Austin's *Pride and Prejudice* (1813), Lydia is Elizabeth Bennett's youngest sister who elopes with Wickham.

LYNETTE (f) The medieval French form of the Celtic *Eluned*, 'idol, icon'. The name, variously spelt Linnet, Linnette, Lynette and Lynnette, became familiar after the publication in 1859 of Tennyson's *Idylls of the King*. The linnet is a small songbird of the finch family, called a linty, and this has been used as a pet name, as well as a description of a Scottish songstress. Short forms are Lyn, Lynn and Lynne.

LYNSEY (f) A popular feminine form of LINDSAY.

M

MABEL (f) A short form of AMABEL, and became more popular, although not now prolific. Amabel has occasionally been confused with ANNABEL. In Scott's *Redgauntlet*, Mabel Moffat is the elderly woman who served the Laird of Solway Lochs in Brokenburn. Variants are Mabelle, Maybel, Maybell and Maybelle, but those names have gone out of fashion.

MADELINE (f) Derived from Madeleine, the French form of MAGDALENE. Madeline (1796–1858), daughter of Sir David Carnegie, 4th Baronet of Southesk, married in 1816, Sir Andrew Agnew, 7th Baronet of Lochnaw. A granddaughter, Madeline Mary, died in 1942. The actress Madeleine Carroll (Marie Bernadette O'Carroll, 1906–87) who was of Irish extraction, kept the name before the public in the 1930s and '40s. The spelling Madeleine is currently more popular in Scotland than Madeline.

MADGE *See* MARJORIE.

MAEVE (f) An Irish form of MAUD.

MAGDALEN, MAGDALENE (f) Heb., 'woman of Magdala', a town on the Sea of Galilee. The biblical Mary Magdalene, who was a witness to the crucifixion and the resurrection of Christ, became the prototype of the reformed prostitute (NT, Matthew 27:61; Mark 15:40; Luke 8:2). The form MADELINE, derived from the French Madeleine, which is of interest, Madeleine de Valois, eldest daughter of Francis I of France, having married (as his first wife) James V, King of Scots, in 1536–37. Lady Magdalene Carnegie, daughter of the Earl of Northesk, married the 1st Marquess of Montrose in 1629, and was mother of the celebrated John Graham of Claverhouse. Madelon appears as wife of Le Jeunesse in Scott's *Quentin Durward*, and in his novel *The Abbot*, Magdalen Graeme appears. Recorded variants are Maudlin and Madelon, and Lena is a pet name.

MAGNUS (m) Lat., 'great'. The name spread through the influence of the Emperor Charlemange, 'Carolus Magnus'. Admirers took Magnus as a personal name, and St Olaf of Norway named a son Magnus. The name travelled to Iceland, Orkney and Shetland, and to Ireland, where it became Mànus; hence the surname McManus. Magnus, called Earl of Caithness in 1232, was probably a son of Gilchrist, Earl of Angus, by a Norwegian mother. Magnus was the name of four earls, all descendants. Magnus Burgher, in Marwick, Birsay, Mainland, Orkney is recorded in 1492. The testament of Magnus Coupland in Hensbuster, Holm, Orkney was confirmed in 1612; that of Magnus Manson of Olstay, Yell, Shetland in 1613. The name has been in regular use, and a recent increase is probably due to author and TV personality Magnus Magnusson, born in Iceland and educated in Edinburgh, former quizmaster in *Mastermind*. The Gaelic form in Scotland, as in Ireland, is Mànus.

MAISIE (f) Usually a pet form of MARJORY, and often

in common speech rendered Mysie. It has occasionally been applied to MARY. Mysie Happer is the miller's daughter, 'a dark-eyed, laughter-loving wench', in Scott's novel, *The Monastery*, and in his *Bride of Lammermoor* Mysie is the sole female domestic at Wolf's Crag.

MALCOLM (m) Gael. *Maol Caluim*, 'servant of [St] Columba'. It appears also in old records as Malcolumb and Malcolium. Malcolm was the name of four kings of the Scots – Malcolm I, son of Donald, reigned in Dalriada, 942–54; Malcolm II, son of Kenneth reigned over the united Scots and Picts, 1005–34; Malcolm III, son of Donald, and called Canmore, 'great head', reigned 1057–93; and Malcolm IV, a boy in his twelfth year when he succeeded his grandfather, David I, reigned 1153–65. The name has been popular in England as well as Scotland, perhaps because of the Saxon lineage of Margaret, Queen of Malcolm Canmore. Malcolm MacPherson (1828–98), a famous piper, composed 'the Lament for Cluny Macpherson', after his chief died in 1885. Sir Malcolm Campbell, 1885–1948, set various speed records on land and water. Callum is a variant.

MALISE (m) Gael. *Mael-Iosa*, 'servant of Jesus'. The name was much favoured by the ancient Earls of Strathearn, who were Grahams. The first so-named was witness to a charter to the church of Dunfermline in 1182. Malise, a tanist of the MacLeans, is said to have had the name given to him as an *ainm rathaid*, or 'road name'. It has been used as a surname and appears today as Mellis. See also GILLIES.

MALVINA (f) Gael. *Malamhin*, said to mean 'smooth brow'. The name was invented by James Macpherson in the eighteenth century. Malvina, daughter of Ossian, is said to have stained the heather white with her tears when she heard of the death in battle of Oscar, her husband. Curiously, white heather is said to be lucky. The name came into general use as Melvina. The male name MELVIN possibly derives for it.

MARC *See* MARK.

MARGARET (f) Gr., from a word, perhaps originally Persian, meaning 'pearl'. It was the name of a third-century saint of Antioch, of whom little is known, and was made famous in Scotland through the Saxon Princess Margaret, daughter of Edward the Exile, who came to Scotland and in 1057 married Malcolm III, King of Scots. She died in 1093 and was canonised. Margaret, Princess of Norway (1282–90), called 'The Maid of Norway', was daughter of King Erik of Norway and Margaret, daughter of Alexander III, of Scotland, by Margaret, daughter of Henry III of England. She was acknowledged as heir to the throne of Scotland in 1284 and succeeded her grandfather, but died near the Orkneys on her way to Scotland. This sad event caused the great competition for the crown, eventually awarded to John Balliol. Two other Scottish queens were called Margaret: Margaret Drummond was the wife of King David II, and died *c.* 1375; Margaret Tudor (1489–1541), daughter of Henry VII of England, married James V of Scotland in 1503. A Kirkcudbright lass, Margaret Chalmers (1763–1843), inspired the poet

Burns to pen two love songs. She married Lewis Hay, a banker, and died at Berne in Switzerland. The name Margaret became so common that Charlotte Yonge (1823–1901), who wrote a *History of Christian Names* (2 volumes, 1863), referred to it as 'the national Scottish female name'. In spite of the fact that HRH Princess Margaret Rose (later Countess of Snowdon) was born at Glamis Castle in Scotland in 1930, the name has steadily lost its popularity, and is now outwith the top one hundred girls' names. Marguerite, the French form, is even less fashionable. Variants are MARGERY, Margo, and MADGE. Pet names are Maggs, Meg, Meggie, Meta, Daisy, Peg, Peggy and Greta, the latter made famous by the film star, Greta Garbo (Greta Lovisa Gustaffson, 1905–90). Occasionally Maisie or Mysie is also a pet name. The Gaelic form of the name is *Mairearad*.

MARGERY (f) A variant of MARGARET, rendered in Gaelic *Marsail*. In Scott's novel *The Heart of Midlothian*, Margery Kittleside is one of Reuben Butler's parishioners. She and Rory MacRand 'southered sin wi' marriage'.

MARGO *See* MARGARET.

MARGUERITE (f) With Margerie, a French form of MARGARET. It is also a flower name, and came into use about the same time as Daisy. Short forms are Margie, Retta and Rita, and the Gaelic style is *Marsali. See also* MARJORIE.

MARIANNE (f) Supposed by many to be a French form of Marie and Anne, but this is doubtful. It seems cognate with MARION or Marian. 'Marian' is a term used in connection with the mother of Jesus, Queen Mary [Tudor] of England and Mary, Queen of Scots, eg, 'The Marian Controversy'. The Elie, Fife, *Old Parochial Register* (1773–1819) records the baptism of Marianne, daughter of William Taylor and Euphemia Wallace, and a note by the clerk states it was said to be derived from Mariamne, wife of Herod the Great.

MARIE (f) A French form of MARY, made famous by the maids of honour of Mary, Queen of Scots. One of the 'Four Maries', a daughter of Lord Seton shared the captivity of her royal mistress in England, and after the execution in 1587 entered a French convent. The other three Maries were Beaton, Fleming and Livingston. Marie is the Latin form. Maria Banks Riddell (1772–1808), of Goldilea, Dumfries, was a friend of the poet Burns, regarding whom she wrote a *Memoir*.

MARINA (f) Lat. feminine form of *Marinus*. It was not much used in Scotland before 1934, when Princess Marina of Greece (d. 1968), married HRH Prince George, Duke of Kent and Earl of St Andrews.

MARION, MARIAN (f) Appears to be cognate with MARIANNE. The name was common in the Middle Ages. Marion, daughter of Sir David Murray of Tullibardine, married Sir Malcolm Drummond of Cargill in 1445. Another Marion Murray, daughter of Cuthbert of Cockpool, married Thomas Kirkpatrick of Closeburn (died 1515), but was divorced from him and her dowry repaid. In Scott's novel, *The Bride of Lammermoor*, Marion Lightbody is an old friend of

Caleb Balderstone. Mairn is a pet name. In Gaeldom, Marian or Marion is synonymous with *Muireall* (See MURIEL).

MARIOTA (f) An obsolete but historic name, once prolific in Scotland. It may have derived from Marriot, recorded in England in the late twelfth century, but has been linked with MARION and occasionally with MARGARET. In 1409 Colin Campbell of Lochawe married his cousin, 'Mariota or Margaret', daughter of John, son of Dugal Campbell. However, it does seem that Mariota gave way to Marion. Robert Arbuthnott of Arbuthnott married *c.* 1475, 'Mariot or Marion', daughter of Sir James Scrimgeour or Dudhope. Again, in the same family, 'Mariota or Marian', her granddaughter, married James Bisset of Easter Kinneff after 1535.

MARJORIE (f) Derived from Margerie, a variant of the French MARGUERITE. King William the Lion had a daughter Marjorie, who married in 1235, Gilbert, Earl of Pembroke, at Berwick. Marjorie, Countess of Carrick in her own right, wife of Robert de Brus, was mother of Robert I, King of Scots, 1306–29, who named a daughter Marjorie. She married Walter, High Stewart of Scotland (1292–1326), and their son John, called Robert, was the first of the Stewart kings. The name, which has enjoyed regular use, is rendered *Marsali* in Gaelic. *Marsali*, daughter of Hugh Cameron of Ariundle, Loch Suinart, was born before 1690. Pet forms are Marge, Margi, and occasionally MADGE.

MARK (m) Lat., from *Mars*, the Roman god of war. It

was, moreover, a personal name, and that of a Roman family. The Gospel of the biblical Mark, evangelist and saint, has been placed second in the *New Testament*, but some scholars claim it is the oldest written account of the ministry of Christ, and dates from *c.* AD 70. In the Middle Ages Venetian merchants obtained his relics and took them to Venice, where they built a basilica in his honour. The bankers of Europe stamped their coins with a winged lion, the symbol of St Mark, and called a 'mark'. There was a King Mark in Arthurian legend. The name was not widely used until after the Reformation. It was favoured by the Ker family, Earls and Marquesses of Lothian, and also occurs in the Home family. It is now very popular, within the top fifteen boys' names. The variant Marc is also popular. Other spellings are Marco and Markus. The Gaelic form, *Marcies*, is not unlike the original Roman *Marcus*.

MARMADUKE (m) Of uncertain origin, but possibly derived from the Irish Maelmaedoc, 'servant of Madoc'. The influence of the Normans on the language gave rise to *Marmaduc*, found in Yorkshire in the sixteenth century. It is now uncommon. Marmaduke Constable-Maxwell (1760–1819) of Everingham, Yorkshire, owned the estate of Terregles in Galloway. His mother, Winifred Maxwell, daughter of the 6th Earl of Nithsdale, was a friend of the poet Burns. The name Marmaduke was continued in that family for another two generations, but Marmaduke Constable-Maxwell, Lord Herries, died without issue in 1908.

MARSALI *See* MARJORIE.

MARTHA (f) The Aramiac feminine form of *Mar*, 'lord', and interpreted as 'lady of the house'. The biblical Martha (NT, Luke 10:38–42) lived in the house of Simon the Leper, and was always busy with household duties. The name was not in common use in Scotland until the sixteenth century. Martha, daughter of Sir James Carmichael, Baronet (1579–1672), married John Kennedy of Kirkmichael. The name is used several times by Scott in the Waverley novels. Pet forms are Marti, Martie, Marty, Mattie and Matty. The Gaelic form is *Moireach*, with Patty as a pet name.

MARTIN (m) Lat. derived from *Martinus*, a diminutive of *Martius*, the god of war, and therefore cognate with MARK. The name was prolific among the early Christians and honoured by the name of the fourth-century St Martin of Tours. It has been used as a surname in Scotland, and in some cases may be a curtailment of MacMartin, a name once prolific in Lochaber. MacMhartainn is simply 'son of the servant of St Martin'. Martin was the name of several popes. In 1342 Martin de Ergail was elected Bishop of Argyll. Robert Martyne was vicar at Garwok in 1497, and there was an old family of the name in St Andrews in the fifteenth century. The use of the name as both forename and surname is apparent in the name of Martin Martin, the Skye historian, whose best-known work is his *Description of the Western Isles of Scotland* (1703). Martin Elliott, 'noted in Border story and song', appears in Scott's novel, *The Black Dwarf*. Martyn is a variant and the Gaelic form is *Mhartainn*. Pet names

are Mart and Marty, and the usual feminine form is
MARTINE.

MARTINE (f) Fr. feminine form of MARTIN. Martina
is a variant made famous by the great tennis star,
Martina Navratilova. Marty is a pet name, used also
for MARTHA.

MARY (f) Heb., probably from *rama*, 'high', 'longed for',
with the prefix *ma* giving 'wished-for child'. The name
is cognate with Miriam, perhaps the older form. Mary,
the scriptural mother of Jesus, Mary Magdalene, and
Mary of Bethany all appear in the New Testament.
The first is usually thought of as the Virgin Mary, but
there is widespread ignorance among Roman Catholics
about the so-called 'immaculate conception'. It is in
fact the dogma (official since 1854) that holds Mary to
have been free of sin from the moment of conception
in the womb of her mother. She was the wife of Joseph,
descended from the royal line of DAVID (NT, Matthew
1:1–16). Her own parents are not recorded in the
canonical gospels, but are named as Joachim and Ann
in the apocryphal *Book of James*. Mary of Magdala is
the prototype of the reformed prostitute, and Mary of
Bethany may be the woman who poured precious oil
over the head of Jesus and wiped his feet with her hair
(NT, Matthew 26:7–12). The best-known Scottish
Mary was the beautiful but unfortunate Queen of
Scots, who lived 1542–87, and was married three times.
Her son James VI of Scotland acceded to the throne
of England in 1603. The poet Burns was associated
with at least three Marys. Mary or May Cameron, an

Edinburgh lass, bore him a child in 1787. 'Highland Mary' Campbell (1763–86), probably born at Dunoon, inspired two songs, and died at Greenock, probably in childbirth. Mary (Polly Stewart, 1775–1847) is the subject of another song. Mary Slessor (1848–1915), born at Aberdeen, was a missionary in Calabar, and Mary Garden (1874–1967), also from Aberdeen, became a famous opera singer in America. The French form MARIE is almost as much used as Mary, but all forms of the name, including Marilyn, MAUREEN, MIRIAM, MOIRA and Marriet, have lost ground in recent years. Pet forms are Molly, Polly, Minnie, Mami, and occasionally Maisie. The Gaelic form is Mairi.

MATILDA (f) O.G. *math hildis*, 'mighty in battle'. The introduction of the name to Britain is due to William the Conqueror, who married Matilda of Flanders. This was an important event, considering that he was a bastard, and it made it possible for him to hold land outside Normandy and also resulted in Flemish knights in his army. The name came early to Scotland, as David II (1124–53) married MAUD or Matilda, Countess of Northampton. The name was long prominent in the blood royal and among titled families. Robert I, King of Scots, married as his second wife, Matilda, daughter of Richard de Burgh, and their eldest son became David II (1324–71). The name lost favour on the accession of the Stewarts. It made a revival in the eighteenth century but is uncommon today. The contracted form of Maud, with the pet name Maudie, is still in use. Other pet names are Mattie, Tilly and Tilda.

MATTHEW (m) Heb. *Mattathiah*. 'gift of God'. Matthew, one of the twelve apostles, was also known as Levi, son of Alphaeus. He was a tax collector in the service of Herod Antipas, but not the Matthew who wrote what has been given as the first gospel. This Matthew, evangelist and saint, was probably a Greek-speaking Jew of Syria, who wrote around AD 75–85. The name was common in the Middle Ages. Matthew [Kinnimond], archdeacon of St Andrews, became Bishop of Aberdeen in 1172. Matthew Scott, chancellor, became Bishop of Dunkeld in 1228 and Matthew [*Machabaeus*] was elected Bishop of Ross in 1272. Matthew Baillie (1761–1823), born at Shotts, was a distinguished anatomist. The name has retained its popularity and is within the top thirty boys' names in Scotland. Mathew is a variant, still in use, and short forms are Matt and Mattie. *Mata* is the Gaelic form.

MAUD, MAUDE (f) The name is synonymous with MATILDA, but also appears as a surname in England. The veteran steam engine *Maude*, No. 65243, which saw service in France during the First World War, was named after General Sir F.S. Maud. It is now owned by the Scottish Railway Preservation Society, Bo'ness and Falkirk. Maude Adams (Maude Kiskadden, 1872–1953) was a famous American stage actress.

MAUREEN (f) Irish Gael., from *Mairin*, a pet form of Mhairi or Mairi. Muirenn, daughter of Cellach Cualann, and sister of St Kentigern of Loch Lomond, was wife of Irgalach, who was cursed by St Adamnan for killing his cousin Niall in 701. She died in 748. According to legend, Queen Finch, consort of Hungus, King of the Picts, who died in 761, had a child called Mouren. The Irish-born stage and screen actress Maureen O'Hara, born 1921, kept the name before the public with memorable performances in films with John Wayne, notably *The Quiet Man* (1952). Moira and Moyra are sometimes anglicised forms of the name.

MAURICE (m) Lat., *Mauritius*, 'a Moor'. This was the name of a third-century Swiss martyr from whom St Moritz derived its name. The Normans brought the name to England, and in 1086 Maurice was Bishop of London. The name appears also as Meurice and later as Morris, which became a surname. Maurice, Abbot of Inchaffray, was present at the Battle of Bannockburn in 1314, and became Bishop of Dunblane. Maurice, second son of Malcolm Drummond of Dronan, Perthshire, was forester of Strathearn, and died in 1346. Admitted burgess of Edinburgh in 1665 was Maurice Trent. Maurice Lindsay is a well-known Scottish author and poet. In Ireland the name became Moriarty. The Scottish Gaelic form is *Maolmuire* or *Gille Moire*. Short forms of Maurice are Moss and Maurie, the latter popular in Australia.

MEG (f) A pet form of MARGARET. Meg Hyslop was landlady at the Globe Tavern in Dumfries, a favourite 'howff' of Robert Burns. She was an aunt of Anna Park, who bore the poet a daughter Elizabeth (1791–1873), who received when she was twenty-one, £200 from the fund raised by her father's admirers. In Scott's *St Ronan's Well*, Meg Dods is the landlady of the

Cleukum Inn, and in his *Guy Mannering* Meg Merilees is a gypsie queen. An old canon at Edinburgh Castle is called 'Mons Meg'. It is thought to have been forged locally for the siege of Threave, 1455, but may have been imported from Flanders.

MEGAN (f) Derived from Meggie, a Welsh diminutive of MARGARET. Welshman David Lloyd George, Prime Minister, 1916–22, named a daughter Megan, and, while the name is considered Welsh, its use spread to other countries. It is currently within the top ten girls' names registered annually in Scotland. Variants are Meghan, Meagan and Meaghan.

MELANIE (f) Gr., meaning 'dark complexioned'. The earliest known form was Melania, borne by two saints, and the name was known to the Romans as well as to the Greeks. It came to Britain from France in the mid seventeenth century. Arthur Ceasar Murray (1797–1848), of the Dysart family, had a daughter Melanie Sophia, who married in 1849, M. Raymond Louis Abrial, of Montalban in France. Melanie Hamilton, featured in Margaret Mitchell's *Gone with the Wind*, brought the name into fashion in several English-speaking countries. Melanie Neef is currently one of Scotland's top track athletes. Mel is a pet name.

MELISSA (f) Gr., 'bee'. The name was personal in early Greece. It was the name of a nymph, also the legendary woman murdered by her husband, Periander, ruler of Corinth, who wandered naked in the underworld, her funeral clothes having been ceremonially burned. The name was favoured by Italian poets in the sixteenth century and in Britain in the nineteenth by Dickens and Tennyson. It was also used by Gilbert and Sullivan in *Princess Ida* (1884). They probably influenced its use as it has risen to within the top fifty names in Scotland. Variant forms are Mellissa, Melisa and Mellisa. It shares the pet name Mel with MELANIE, and occasionally Liza with ELIZABETH.

MELVILLE (m) The name is territorial, from the barony of Malaville in Normandy. Galfridus de Melveill witnessed a charter by King Malcolm IV, and also appears in documents of the reign of William the Lion. The lands of Melville near Dalkeith were one of the early possessions of the family, as well as Melville in Fife. James Melville the Reformer, spelt his own name Melville and Melvin, even on the same page. There are numerous variants on record, including Meluide, Malvene, Mellwell and Melvyne. Its use as a forename is less widespread.

MELVIN (m) Said to be a back formation of MALVINA, but (see above) is often a variant of MELVILLE. It may occasionally be derived from an Irish form meaning 'polished chief'.

MHAIRI, MAIRI (f) The Gaelic form of MARY.

MICHAEL (m) Heb., a personal name meaning 'who is like God'. It is synonymous with Miciah or Micah, and was the name of an eighth-century prophet; also of the young man noted in the scriptures (OT, Judges 17:1–3) as owning up to his mother the theft from her of 1,100 shekels of silver. One of the seven archangels was Michael, a leader in battle. The name was prolific in the Middle Ages. Michael, a Manx monk, became Bishop of the Isles, and died about 1203. Michael, a friar of Cashel, was made Bishop of the Isles in 1387. About 1307 Michael was Abbot of Cambuskenneth. Michael gave rise to the surname Mitchell, which has also been recorded as a forename, probably through French influence. Michael is one of the Darling children in J.M. Barrie's *Peter Pan*. Short forms are Mike, Mitch, Mick (a generic word for an Irishman), Micky and Michael. The name is still very popular; it is within the top ten boys' names registered annually.

MICHAELA, MICHELLE (f) Although there was one Michal, younger daughter of Saul, who gave her as a wife to DAVID, then removed her and gave her to somebody else (OT, Samuel 19:20–28), Michelle came as a forename from France as a feminine form of MICHAEL, and has the same meaning. Michaela is a much-favoured form, and other variants are Michele and Mikaela. A song by the Beatles, *Michelle*, recorded in the mid-1960s, influenced use of the name.

MILDRED (f) O.E., *milde and thrythe*, 'mild power'. The seventh-century saint, King Merowald of Mercia, had three daughters from one of whom, *Mildthryth*, the name is derived. All three were canonised, leading to the popularity of Mildred in the Middle Ages. The name seems to have gone into decline after the Norman Conquest, but it was revived in the nineteenth century, although never prolific in Scotland. The usual pet name is Milly. In Gaelic the name is rendered *Milread*.

MIRIAM (f) Heb., probably from *ràma*, 'high', 'longed

for', and cognate with MARY. In the scriptures, Miriam is the sister of AARON, and thus half-sister of Moses (OT, Exodus 15:20). She took part in the celebrations of the Israelites after their miraculous crossing of the Red Sea. Recorded variants are Mary, Mariamne and Miryam. The name is sometimes confused with Mira (see MYRA). Jews in Britain have favoured Miriam, and in Scott's *Ivanhoe*, a daughter of the celebrated doctor, Rabbi Manasses of Byzantium, is so named.

MORAG (f) Gael. Equivalent of SARAH, now used independently, but not prolific.

MURIEL (f) Irish Gaelic, *Muirgheal*, 'sea', 'bright'. The name was probably common to Celtic languages, and in Scottish Gaelic *Muireall* is interchangeable with MARION. Derived from it are the surnames Merrall and Murrell. Muriel is found at an early date in the genealogy of the Rose family of Kilravock, and also in that of the Calders of Calder (Cawdor). Muriel, heiress of John Calder, in 1498, when a flame-haired little girl, was placed under the wardship of the 2nd Earl of Argyll, and her removal from her ancestral home to Argyll was effected through bloodshed. Muriella, daughter of Alexander Sutherland, ancestor of the family of Duffus, married Alexander Seton of Meldrum, after 1456. Other variants are Murial and Murielle. Molly is sometimes used as a pet name.

MURRAY (m) This prolific surname is of territorial origin, from the province of Moray, and is of considerable antiquity. William, son of Freskin the Fleming, was styled 'de Moravia' *c*. 1200. William de Morreve swore fealty to Edward I in 1296, and Sir Andrew Moray was styled *panetarius Scotiae* in 1327. The name is borne by a number of titled families. James Stewart, Earl of Moray, was half-brother of Mary, Queen of Scots, and the song 'The Bonnie Earl o' Moray' may have influenced the modern use as a forename. Moray McLaren (1901–71), a journalist and author of Scottish books, married the actress Lennox Milne, OBE.

MYRA (f) Myrra was an Ionian slave, the favourite concubine of Sardanapalus, the Assyrian king, who perished with him on a funeral pile, which she herself lit. However, the more recent forename Myra is said to have been 'invented' by Fulke Greville, Lord Brooke (1554–1628), who wrote amorous verses to a lady whom he so designated in the poems. Mira is a variant. The name is in regular but not wide use in Scotland.

N

NAN (f) Occasionally a diminutive of ANN or ANNA, but also recorded as a pet form of NANCY.

NANCY (f) Usually a diminutive of ANN and the variant spellings, but has long appeared as an independent name. In Scotland Nancy is often interchangeable with AGNES. Burns's 'My Nanie O' was a girl called Agnes Fleming, born 1765, daughter of John Fleming, who farmed in Calcothill, near Lochlea, Tarbolton.

NAOMI (f) Heb. 'pleasant'. In the scriptures Naomi is the
wife of Elimelech and mother-in-law of RUTH. With
her husband and two sons she went from Bethlehem
to Moab (OT, Ruth 1:1–2). Emilelech died and after
her sons Mahlon and Chilion married Moab women.
Naomi intended to return to Bethlehem, but remained
in Moab. Considering the beauty of the name it is curious it was not more popular. It was not much used in
English-speaking countries before the eighteenth century. Naomi, daughter of James Hamilton of Clanbrazil,
in Ireland, married in the early part of the eighteenth
century, Capt. Archibald Murray of the Blackbarony
family. The veteran authoress, the late Naomi Margaret
Mitchison (maiden surname Haldane), Baroness, CBE,
was tribal mother of Bakgatia, Botswana.

NATALIE (f) Lat. *natale domini*, 'birthday of the Lord',
which has come to be reckoned on Christmas day.
St Natalia, wife of St Adrian, who was martyred in the
fourth century, has a place in the calendar of the Greek
church. The spelling has been influenced by the French
Nathalie. Natalia and Nataska are popular names in
Russia. The actress Natalie Wood (Natasha Gurdin,
1938–81) influenced the use of the name, and it is now
very popular. Nat and Nattie are pet names.

NATASHA (f) The Russian form of NATALIE is now
within the top forty girls' names registered annually
in Scotland.

NATHAN (m) Heb. 'gift'. At first sight Nathan seems to be
a short form of NATHANIEL, and occasionally may be
used as such, but it is really a forename in its own right.

In the Bible Nathan was a leading figure at the court of DAVID, and in a contest for the succession between David's sons Adonijah and Solomon, took the part of the latter (OT, 2 Samuel 7:2–29). The name was uncommon in this country until the late seventeenth century. Nathan, elder son of Sir John Maxwell of Calderwood, 3rd Baronet, died in the Darien Disaster, *c.* 1699. Nathan gained ground in the present century and is within the top eighty boys' names. It has also been used as a surname. Nat and Nattie are short forms.

NATHANIEL (m) Heb. 'God has given'. Nathaniel, twice named by JOHN (NT, John 1:45–49) is almost certainly the apostle called Bartholomew by the other evangelists. It came into use in the seventeenth century. Nathaniel Moncrief of Randerston, Fife, lived in the early part of that century, and his daughter Margaret carried the name into the Spens family of Lathallan. The name is currently less popular than NATHAN, and shares the same pet forms.

NEIL (m) Irish Gaelic, from *Nia*, or *Naddh*, 'champion'. Niall, stemming from the Norse *Njal* and *Njall*, was favoured in Ireland from the time of Niall of the Nine Hostages, who ruled at Tara around AD 400. Neil has been used as both forename and surname, and there are reasonable grounds for accepting that the MacNeils descend from him, and *Aedh Athaeuch*. Neil Og was chief of the MacNeils in the regin of Robert I. Another Neil Og MacNeil of Barra fought at Worcester in 1651. The Latin form is *Nigelus* or *Nigellus*, and the forms Nygell and Nigel became popular in the later

Middle Ages. Nigello *capellano* witnessed a confirmation by Robert, Bishop of Glasgow, in 1150. Neil Gow (1727–1807) was a famous Scots fiddler whose portrait was painted by Raeburn. Neil Munro (1864–1930) and Neil Gunn (1891–1974) were leading Scottish novelists. Several forms of the name are in use today: Neil, Neill, Neal, Neale, Niel and Nigel, the first being the most prolific. Niall is the Gaelic form, and Neilie is a pet name.

NICHOLAS (m) Lat. *Nicolaus*, from a Gr. compound word meaning 'victory of the people'. Nicholas, a proselyte of Antioch, appears as a deacon in the scriptures (NT, Acts 6:5). St Nicholas, Bishop of Myra, AD 300, is regarded as the patron saint of children, sailors, pawnbrokers and wolves. The name, venerated in the Eastern and Western churches, reached England before 1066, and was known in Scotland by the twelfth century. Many clerics bore the name. Nicholas, prior of Scone, is on record in 1128. Nicholas, sub-dean of Brechin, was consecrated bishop there in 1294. Nicholas Hude, arrow-maker, made thirty-two sheaves for the king in 1438. Current variant forms of the name are Nicolas and Nikolas, with Nicki, Nicky, Nikki and Nico as diminutives. The Gaelic form is *Neacal*, and the feminine rendering is NICOLA or NICOLE. Nicholas appears also as a surname.

NICOLA (f) This is the Italian feminine form of NICHOLAS, and was known in England as early as the reign of King John (1199–1216). It came later to Scotland. Nicola, daughter of Sir George Bruce of Carnock, married Sir

John Arnot of Fernie in 1641. Nicolette is the French form. Nicole was a favourite name among the Gordons of Upper Deeside. Variants are Nichola and Nichole, and pet forms are Colette, Niki, Nikkie and Nikky.

NIGEL (m) Derived from the Latin form of NEIL, and used anciently in Scotland. Nigel was cook to King William the Lion (1165–1214). Nigel Tranter was Scotland's most prolific historical novelist.

NINA (f) A Russian diminutive of ANNE, used occasionally since the middle of the nineteenth century. It is becoming more popular.

NINIAN (f) Ninian or Ninius was a saint of British origin, educated at Rome, who founded a monastery at *Candida Casa*, 'The White House', in Wigtownshire, *c*. AD 400. He is said to have converted the Southern Picts to Christianity. The name is probably cognate with Nennius, the name of an eighth-century British historian, and with the Irish Ninidh. For a time Ninian was a forename common in Northumberland and Yorkshire, but it came to be almost entirely Scottish. Ninian Stewart of Ardmaleish and Greenan was Sheriff of Bute around 1490. Ninian, 3rd Lord Ross of Halkhead, was an ambassador to France in 1515. The rector of the High School of Linlithgow at the Reformation was Ninian Winzet (*c*. 1518–92), who distinguished himself in the defence of the Roman church, against John Knox. Ninian Home of Paxton, Governor of Grenada, was murdered there in 1795. The Gaelic form of the name is *Ringeam*. Nein is a pet name.

NORA (f) A pet form of Eleanora (*See* ELEANOR), sometimes rendered Norah, as in Ibsen's play, *A Doll's House*. The wife of Noah was *Noraidh*, mother of Shem, Ham and Japheth (OT, Genesis 5:32). Norah is the favoured variant in Scotland and Ireland. Recorded pet names are Noey and Onney.

NORMAN (m) O.E., 'north-man', and cognate with the O.G. *Nordemann*. The name was known in England before the Conquest, and became a surname. It went into decline in England as a forename, but in its Gaelic form, Tormod, survived in the north and north-west. Tormod, son of Leod, married Fingula MacCrotan, and their son, who succeeded his grandfather, was the ancestor of the MacLeods of Harris, Dunvegan and Glenelg. Norman was the name of six chiefs of Clan MacLeod. Norman, second son of Sir Alexander of Dunbar of Cumnock, Ayrshire, is mentioned in writs, *c.* 1550. The name is in regular, but not wide, use. Pet names are Norm and Norrie.

O

OCHTREDA (f) *See* UCHTRED

OLAUS (m) 'progenitor'. A Latin form of O.Nor. *Olafr*.It is synonymous with Olave, which appears as Olaf, Olef, Olof and Oliet. Olaus II, King of Norway, born 984, 1026–30, was called 'St Olaf the Double Beard'. Leod, son of Olaf the Black, King of Man and the Isles, had a fourth son, Olaus, who went to Arran, and is said to have been the progenitor of Fullertons there. The name was favoured by some branches of Clan MacLeod. Olaus, son of Norman MacLeod of Glenelg, emigrated with his wife and family to Ontario, Canada, in 1817.

OLIVE (f) Lat. *oliva*, 'olive', used as a personal name. St Oliva was a Roman virgin martyr of Anagi, and another St Oliva was famed as the protector of the olive crops of Italy. The name appears in England in the twelfth century, usually as *Oliff*. Shakespeare favoured *Olivia* in *Twelfth Night*, and Olive came into fashion in the eighteenth century. It was used by Goldsmith in *The Vicar of Wakefield* (1766). Olivia is now the usual form in Scotland. The award-winning actress Olivia de Havilland, whose film career began in 1935, has probably influenced use of the name. Top Scottish golfer Colin Montgomerie has named a daughter Olivia.

OLIVER (m) Fr. *Olivier*, *'fabricant ou marchant d'olive'*, is the source of this name. It was the name of one of Charlemange's peers, but possibly the name was associated with the Norse *Olaf*. The name appears as both forename and surname. Walter Olifer witnessed a gift of the serf *Gillemachoi de Conglud* to the Bishop of Glasgow, *c.* 1180. Olyver, son of Kyluert, was a follower of the Earl of March at the close of the twelfth century. The name was well used in Scotland until Oliver Cromwell's 'Protectorate', in the middle of the seventeenth century, when it lost favour, except as a surname in some Border counties. The Christian name was revived in the nineteenth century. Oliver Wendell

Holmes (1809–94), the American poet and writer, was of Scots descent. The Gaelic form of the name is *Olaghair* or *Olibreis*. Diminutives are Noll, Nolly and Ollie.

OONAGH (f) The etymology is obscure, but Oona and Oonagh are certainly of Irish origin, perhaps from *Abhainn* (OWEN or Eoghan). Juno is another Irish form. In O.Nor. UNA is a first name for a girl, meaning 'content'. The name has frequently been anglicised as WINIFRED or translated as AGNES from a fancied link with the Latin *agnus* and the Gaelic *uan*, 'lamb'. Oonagh, wife of the immortal Charlie Chaplin, probably gave the name a boost in the 1950s and '60s.

OSWALD (m) O.E. compound *Osweald*, from *os*, 'a God', and *weald*, 'power', usually interpreted as 'power of God'. Oswald, King of Northumbria, was killed fighting the Welsh at Oswestry in 642. He was canonised and the place was named after him. A second St Oswald helped St Dunstan with church reforms in the late tenth century. In time Oswald became a surname, as did the similar Norman name of Osmond. Oswald was a popular Christian name in the later Middle Ages. The Oswalds of Cairhness descend from James Oswald of Kirkwall, who died *c.* 1630. There were land-owning families of the name in Fife. James Oswald (1715–69) was a political writer, using the pen name Sylvester Otway. The name is now uncommon. Ossie is a pet name.

OWEN (m) The name was known anciently in Ireland and Wales (where it is still popular), and the roots are probably Celtic. Some writers make it a form of Latin *Eugenius*. In Ireland it was rendered Eoghan, and Niall of the Nine Hostages had a son of this name, sometimes called Owen, who died in 465. The name was carried to the Scottish Dalriada, where Eoghan, son of Angus, ruled for fourteen years and in 836 Uven, son of Unuist (Hungus), was King of the Southern Picts. In Strathclyde, where the language was allied to the Welsh, Owen 'The Bald', son of Domhnall, was killed in battle *c.* 1018. In Wales Owen Glendower fought for independence in the fifteenth century. The Scottish Gaels use the old Irish form of Eoghan. Owen is a surname, also Owenson. Robert Owen (1771–1858) carried out social experiments at New Lanark, and his son Robert Dale Owen (1801–77), emigrated to America, where he was an author and politician. Owena has appeared in Wales as a feminine Christian name.

P

PAMELA (f) A derivation from Gr., meaning 'all honey', is possible, but the name was first used by Sir Philip Sidney (1554–86) in his romance *Arcadia*, published in 1590. It was not in general use until after Samuel Richardson (1689–1761) used it as the name of his servant girl, Pamela Anderson, in his novel *Pamela*

(1740). The name is within the top seventy girls' names used in Scotland. Pam, a pet form, is occasionally used as a name in its own right.

PATRICIA (f) Lat. feminine form of *Patricius*, 'noble'. There was a seventh-century nun, St Patricius, patron of Naples. Its use as a female Christian name continued sporadically until the beginning of the eighteenth century. Patricia became a popular name after Princess Victoria Patricia Helen Elizabeth, born 1886, daughter of Arthur William, Duke of Connaught, son of Queen Victoria, began to appear in public life, and in 1918 married into the Scottish noble family of Ramsay of Dalhousie. Pet forms of Patricia are Pat, Patty, Paddy, Trish and Trishia. The last two appear infrequently as independent names.

PATRICK (m) Lat. *Patricius*, a patrician, usually described as 'nobleman'. The early Latin life of St Patrick, said to have been born in Scotland, also gives him the name *Cothraige*, by which he was known during his slavery in Ireland. After his escape he sought to convert the Irish to Christianity. The Irish thought the name too sacred for common use, and it did not become prolific until after the Plantation of Ulster by Scottish families in the early part of the seventeenth century. Several landed families in Scotland favoured the forename of Patrick, among them the Humes of Marchmont and the Houstons of Houston, both from the fifteenth century. In Scottish Gaelic the name is found in four forms: *Pàdruig*, with 't' and 'c' unaspirated, but reduced to the corresponding mediae; *Pàruig* for *Pàthruig*, in which the 't' has been aspirated, consequently lost and 'c' made into medial 'g'; *Para*, a pet or short form of the last; and *Pàdair* or *Pàtair*, which was a form of Patrick in Arran and Kintyre. The last form enters into combination with *cill*, 'a church', in *Cill Phadair*, the Gaelic name of Kilpatrick. The name has thus been confused with PETER, and the two names are often synonymous. Patrick is also a surname, and an old family so called had some link with Kilwinning Abbey. With *gille*, it gives *Gillepatrick*, hence MacPhatrick and Paterson. Diminutives are Pat and Paddy, the latter (like Mick) frequently used as a generic name for an Irishman.

PAUL (m) Lat., *paulus*, 'small'. The biblical Paul, previously Saul, was a missionary, tentmaker, martyr and saint: next to Jesus the most important figure in Christianity. His fame rests on his journeys and his faith, and he is the patron saint of preachers and tentmakers. There were several popes named Paul. The use of the name in medieval England brought out surnames like Pole and Powell. It came early to Scotland. Paul, Earl of Orkney, on the death of his brother Harold, *c.* 1140, obtained possession of Caithness, but the Norwegian king caused the province to be divided between Paul and his cousin Kali. Paul Balkeson, who died in 1251, was sheriff of Skye and foster father of Leod, progenitor of the MacLeods. The name came more into use after the Reformation, and appears also as a surname. Patrick Paul was a witness at Tuliboil in 1546, and Alexander Paul, merchant in Elgin, is on record in 1696. John Paul (1747–92), born at Arbigland, Kirkbean parish, was the virtual founder of the American navy, and added Jones to his name. In Gaelic the name is rendered *Pal* or *Pol*. There are several feminine forms.

PAULA, PAULINE (f) Feminine forms of PAUL. There was a fourth-century saint named St Paula, who pioneered several convents in Bethlehem and was remembered in the Middle Ages. Pauline and Paulene are respectively Latin and French forms. Other variants are Pauline and Paulette, but these are less popular than Paula, which is within the top one hundred girls' names registered annually in Scotland. Polly is occasionally used as a pet name.

PEGGY (f) A favourite pet name for MARGARET. Peggy Alison was the supposed heroine of Burns's song, 'Bonny Peggy Alison', but the original was probably Alison Begbie, the 'Lass of Cessnock Banks'.

PENELOPE (f) Gr., from a word meaning 'reel' or 'bobbin', by which 'a weaver', may be the best interpretation. In Homer's *Odysseus*, Penelope was the name of the wife of Odysseus, who waited ten years for her husband to return from the Trojan War. The name has been in regular use in Britain since the sixteenth century. Penelope Devereux (1562–1607), daughter of William, Earl of Essex, was the Stella of Sir Philip Sidney, and travelled with him to Ireland. In that country the name was often interchangeable with Fionnghuala (See FENELLA). Lady Penelope Chrichton succeeded her brother William, 3rd Earl of Dumfries, who died unmarried in 1694, and married her cousin, William Dalrymple of Dunure. The name appears in later generations. Penelope is a popular name for a chaste wife. It has been popularised in recent years by the actress Penelope Keith. Pennie and Penney are infrequent variants. Penny is the usual pet name, but in Scotland at least, has been recorded independently.

PENUEL (m, f) A rare Christian name of uncertain origin, which was used as masculine in the scriptures. Panuel, son of Hur, was the father of Gedor (OT, 1 Chronicles, 4:4). The name came into the Colquhoun family of Luss before 1669, when Penuel, daughter of James Cunningham of Ballyachen, Donegal, Ireland, married Sir James Colquhoun, 4th Baronet. Penuel (1719–98) daughter of Sir James Colquhoun or Grant, and Ann Colquhoun of Luss, married in 1740, Capt. Alexander Grant of Ballindalloch. Later examples appear among the Grants (later Ogilvie-Grants), notably Penuel (1750–1835), daughter of Sir Ludovic Grant, who married Henry Mackenzie (1745–1831) author of *The Man of Feeling* (1771).

PETER (m) Gr., 'rock'. Peter the apostle was the legendary founder of the Church of Rome. His name was Simon, a Galilean fisherman, but he was given the name Peter or Cephas, meaning 'rock' in Hebrew as well as Greek. He was the 'rock' on which Jesus chose to build his Church. His name was popular throughout Christendom. The Normans introduced the French form Piers, the use of which declined in the fourteenth century. Petrus was the Latin form used in official documents. Petrus de Haga, ancestor of the Haigs of Bemersyde, granted a charter of the forest of Flatwood to the Abbey of Dryburgh, *c.* 1240. In Scotland the name was frowned upon after the Reformation as it smacked of papacy, but it returned to fashion in the present century. It was also a surname, and a family of this name was long associated with Glasgow and the Lanarkshire estate of Crossbasket. The Gaelic form of the name is *Peadar*, and the feminine form is PETERINA. *See also* PATRICK.

PETERINA (f) The old feminine form of PETER is now often rendered Petrina, and Trina is a short form. *See* PETRONELLA.

PETRONELLA (f) Lat. diminutive of *Patronius*, the name of a Roman *gens*, and possibly derived from *petra*, 'stone'. It was the name of a first-century martyr and saint, supposed, from an inscription at Rome, to have been a daughter of St Peter. She was invoked against fevers, and the name became common in the Middle Ages, when it was used as a feminine form of PETER. From it at least three surnames evolved: Parnall, Pernell and Parnwell. For some obscure reason, Pernel (now an occasional male name) came to be a generic name for a priest's concubine, and was later applied to any loose woman. Petronilla was a common variant, but both names are now uncommon.

PHILADELPHIA (m, f) Gr., 'brotherly love'. It was the name of a city founded by *Altalus Philadelphus*, King of Pegamus. The angel of the church of Philadelphia is mentioned in the scriptures (NT, Revelations 3:7). At one time Philadelphia was sometimes used as a male name. The Quaker, William Penn (1664–1718) founded Philadelphia, Pennsylvania, from the biblical place-name, and established a liberal government. The poet Burns wrote 'There was a lass and she was fair', for Philadelphia Barbara (1779–1825), second daughter of John McMurdo of Drumlanrig.

PHILIP, PHILLIP (m) Gr. *Philippos*, 'horse lover'. Philip was the name of an apostle (NT, Matthew 10:3) and was much used by early Christians. In medieval times it also became a surname, with several variants. Philip de Keth, as marischal, witnessed a charter by William the Lion before 1199. Philip, Dean of Brechin, is on record *c.* 1350. Philip Guarine, in Scott's novel, *The Betrothed*, was squire to Hugo de Lacy. Phelim is an anglicised form of the name, and Phelyp has also been recorded. Phil is the usual diminutive, and PHILIPPA is the feminine form.

PHILIPPA (f) Lat. feminine form of PHILIP, although in ancient times Philip itself was in use. Philippa, daughter of David of Strathyre, the last Celtic Earl of Atholl, who died *c.* 1370, married Sir Ralph Percy; secondly, Sir John Halsham. The name is still in regular, but not wide use. Pippa is a pet name.

PHOEBE (f) Gr. *Phoibe*, feminine of *phoibos*, 'bright'. In Greek mythology, Phoebe was the goddess of the moon, and sister of Phoebus, the sun god. In the scriptures, Phebe is 'a servant of the church' at Cenchrea (NT, Romans 16:1). Phebe is a shepherdess in Shakespeare's *As You Like It*. The name became much used in Christian countries after the Reformation but was not greatly favoured in Scotland. Phoebe Mayflower is Alice Lee's maid in Scott's *Woodstock*. Variants are Pheobe, Pheable, Pheba, Pheoby, Phobe and Phoeby.

POLLY *See* MARY.

PRIMROSE (f) Usually said to be a flower name, but early examples may derive from the surname Primrose, which is of local origin, from lands in Dunfermline parish, probably meaning 'tree of the moor', and recorded as early as 1387. It is the surname of the Earls of Rosebery, descended from Henry Primrose, who lived in the first half of the sixteenth century. The arms show three primroses. Primrose, daughter of Hon. John Campbell of Mamore, and Elizabeth, daughter of John, 8th Lord Elphinstone, married in 1733, Simon, 11th Lord Lovat, who was executed in 1747. The name probably came from her mother's sister-in-law, Elizabeth, daughter of Sir William Primrose of Carrington. Primrose is a name sometimes given to children born on 29th April – Primrose Day.

PRISCILLA (f) Lat., a diminutive of *prisca*, meaning 'ancient'. The name appears in the Bible (NT, Acts 18:26, and Romans 16:3). It is the name of a saint and was used by the early Christians. The Puritans also favoured the name. Priscilla Begbie was the first wife of the famous Edinburgh clock-maker, Humphrey Milne or Mills (died 1695), who hailed from Staffordshire. The name is not now common. Variants found are Prescilla, Pricilla, Priscella and Prissilla. Pet names are Cilla, Priss and Prissy.

Q

QUENTIN (m) Lat. derived from *quinctus*, 'fifth'. There was a Roman clan of the name, and Quintinus, an early saint, is patron of Kirkmahoe. It was the Normans who brought the name to England, and it became more prolific in Scotland. Quintin Kennedy (1520–64), Abbot of Crossraguel, publicly disputed with John Knox at Maybole on the subject of the sacrifice of the mass. Quenteine Hamilton was admitted burgess and guild-brother of Edinburgh in 1648. The revival of the name in the nineteenth century was probably due to Scott's novel, *Quentin Durward* (1823). The Gaelic form is *Caoidhean*.

R

RACHEL (f) Heb., 'ewe', symbolising 'gentle'. In the scriptures Rachel is the younger and more attractive daughter of Laban, and with her sister LEAH, wife of their cousin Jacob. Rachel was barren, but late in life through divine intervention had two sons, Joseph and Benoni, called Benjamin. She died giving birth to the latter, and was buried at Bethlehem (OT, Genesis 35:17–18)). The name became fashionable after the

Reformation and is very popular today. It jumped from the thirteenth most popular given name in 1990 to the ninth in 1994. The variant Rachael is some way behind, but still favoured. The Spanish form, Raquel, made famous by the Chicago-born actress and sex symbol Raquel Welsh (Raquel Tejeda) does not appear to have influenced Scottish usage. Rachel Ainslie, born 1768, was the charming sister of Robert Ainslie, who accompanied Robert Burns on the first stage of his Border tour in May, 1787. In Scott's *Peveril of the Peak* (1823), Rachel is a girl who acted occasionally as Deborah Debbitche's assistant in attending Alice Bridgenorth and Julian Peverill, when children together at Martindale Castle. *My Cousin Rachel*, a popular novel (1951) by the late Daphne du Maurier, may have had some influence on the use of the name. The variant Rachelle is in current use, and diminutives are Rach, Ray and Rochie. The common Gaelic spelling is *Rachall*.

RALPH (m) Probably O.Fr. In O.E. records it is rendered Radulph and Ralf, and those forms were strengthened after the Norman Conquest. Rauf and Raff appear up to the seventeenth century, when Rafe (now a pet name) became popular. Ralph and Donald, sons of Dunegal, ruled Nithsdale independently of Fergus, Lord of Galloway, about the middle of the twelfth century. Radulphus or Ralph de Vere witnessed a confirmation by William the Lion to the Abbey of Cambuskenneth, *c.* 1199. Ralph, son of Sir John Constable of Burton Constable, ancestor of the Viscounts Dunbar, died before 1577. The name is in regular, but not wide, use.

RANALD (m) *See* REGINALD.

RANDOLPH (m) O.E. *Randwulf*, 'shield-wolf'. A common name in the Middle Ages, usually rendered Ranulf or Randal, the latter giving rise to a number of surnames. The Latin form Radalphus became Randolph, a famous name in Scottish history, also used as a surname. Sir Thomas Randolph, the nephew, and from 1308 the comrade of Bruce, was created Earl of Moray. He recaptured Edinburgh Castle from the English and was regent from the king's death in 1329 until his own in 1332. Randolph, 9th Earl of Galloway (Stewart), had a son Randolph, 11th Earl and a captain in the 42nd Regiment. The late robust actor Randolph Scott, who starred in many western films, helped popularise the name in America. Randy is a pet form.

RAYMOND (m) O.G. compound *ragan-mund*, 'counsel protection'. The name was brought to England by the Normans as Raimond or Reimond, and became Raymond. Ray, a common pet name, is an old Scottish surname and appears in the fifteenth century. Thomas *filius* Ray, witnessed a charter of confirmation by Alexander *filius* Walter, of his father's gift to the Abbey of Paisley in 1239. Raimunde is a feminine form in Germany.

REBECCA (f) Heb., possibly 'heifer'. The biblical Rebekah, 'fair to look upon', was daughter of Bethuel the Syrian, and sister of Laban. She became wife to Isaac, and had twin sons, Esau and Jacob, the younger being her favourite, and upon whom by a ruse she had bestowed Isaac's blessing and inheritance. Pocahontas

(1595–1617), daughter of an Indian chief of Virginia, was rescued by Capt. John Smith when about to be killed by her father. She later married Capt. John Rolfe and was baptised Rebeca. Rebekah Carmichael, a young Scottish poetess, had some verse published in 1790, and Robert Burns subscribed for two copies. The Gaelic form of the name is *Rebecca*, and pet names are Beck, Becky and Reba.

REGINALD (m) O.Nor. *Rognvaldr*, 'counsel power'. Reginald has the same meaning as RANALD, RONALD and ROGNVALD, all names in use in the Highlands and Islands from an early period. Reginald (died 1207), son of Somerled, *regulus* of the Isles, and his wife Ragnhild, daughter of Olaf, King of Man and the Isles, was progenitor of the MacDonalds, Ranald is a highly favoured name in Gaeldom, followed by Ronald. Reginald was much used by the McDonalds and others. Reginald Kirkpatrick was killed at Durham in 1346. The English equivalent is Reynold. Reginald *Macer*, a monk of Melrose, became Bishop of Ross in 1195. It is possible that Reginald or Ranald, the Bishop of the Isles around 1220, was of royal blood. The Ronalds of Ayrshire, especially those of the Bennals, near Tarbolton, feature in the life and work of the poet Burns. A common Gaelic form is *Raonull*. Diminutives of Reginald are Reg, Reggie, Rex and Rennie, while Ronald is shortened to Ron and Ronnie.

REUBEN (m) Heb. 'renewer'. In the scriptures Reuben is the eldest of the twelve sons of Jacob, and his mother was LEAH (OT, Genesis 29:23–32). The name came into use in Britain in the seventeenth century, and has had a recent revival in Scotland, although it is not prolific.

RHIAN (f) Welsh, 'maiden'. The name came into prominence in Wales in the 1950s, and is becoming popular in Scotland, where Rhiann, Rhianna, Rhianne and Rhiannon have been recorded in recent years.

RHODA (f) Gr., *rhoden*, 'rose'. In the scriptures Rhoda is a highly strung girl in the house of MARY, mother of John Mark, where a number of Christians gathered to pray for PETER, apprehended by Herod Agrippa I. Having escaped from his confinement he rapped on the garden door, and was recognised by Rhoda, who, instead of letting him in, ran back into the house with the news (NE, Acts 12:14). The name did not come into use as a British forename before the seventeenth century. It achieved popularity with the publication of *Rhoda Fleming*, a novel by George Meredith (1828–1909) in 1865, but has not been widely used in Scotland.

RHONA (f) The name is of uncertain origin, but possibly from O.Nor. *hraun-ey*, 'rough isle', or is a feminine form of RONAN. It came into use in the nineteenth century about the same time as Rona, which may have the same meaning, or one may be a variant of the other. There are several Scottish islands which might have given rise to the name, the most likely being Rona, between Skye and the Scottish mainland, about 11½ miles north-east of Portree. Watson gives the meaning as O.Nor *hraun-ey*. Another small island called Rona is situated at an equal distance of forty-four miles from the Butt of Lewis and Cape Wrath. On this remote isle was an ancient oratory dedicated to St Ronan, who died in 737. It has long been uninhabited and in 1850 was offered to the government by Sir James Matheson for a penal settlement. An islet off the coast of mainland Shetland is called St Ronan's Isle, and there is an island called Ronay, belonging to North Uist parish, in the Outer Hebrides. St Ronan appears to have been well-known outside Bute, and at Innerleithen, in Peeblesshire, a mineral well was named after him. It provided Scott with the title of a novel (1823).

RICHARD (m) O.G. *ric-heard*, 'hardy ruler', which developed into Ricard. The Normans spread the present form of the name, which was known in Scotland in the twelfth century. Ricardo *capellanis* (chaplain) witnessed a confirmation by the Bishop of St Andrews, in favour of the Abbey of Kelso, 1128. Richard, nephew of Alwyn, Abbot of Holyrood, became Bishop of St Andrews in 1165. The name achieved celebrity in England through Richard I (1157–99), *Cœur de Lion*, and some notoriety from Shakespeare's *Richard III* (1452–85). Richard became also a surname. Alan Richert, a follower of the Earl of Casillis, was respited for murder in 1526. The name had a number of variants, including Richards, Richardson, Rikard and Richie, Richie, Dickie, Dickieson, Dickinson and Dickson, a common Border surname. Pet forms, from which some of the surnames derive, are Richie, Dick, Dickie and Ricky. The name appears in Gaelic as *Ruiscart*, and Richenda has been recorded as a feminine form.

ROBBIE (m) A popular pet form of ROBERT.

ROBERT (m) O.G. compound, *hrothi*, 'fame', and *berhta*, 'bright', giving *Hreodbeort*. The Vikings rendered it *Hrolf*. William the Conqueror was the son of Hrolf 'the Devil', and Harlotta, a tanner's daughter, and his eldest son, the Duke of Normandy, was Robert, who died in 1134. The Brus family, from Brix, near Cherbourg, in Normandy, favoured the name. Robert, son of Adam, fought at Hastings in 1066. His descendant, Robert de Brus, a powerful baron in Yorkshire, was ancestor of Robert I, King of Scots, 1306–29. His son, David II (1316–90), died without issue. His sister Marjory, married Walter the Steward, and their son, Robert II, was the first of the Steward Kings. Robert, a chaplain, became Bishop of Ross in 1219. Robert was the Christian name of several eminent men of the seventeenth century. Robert Adam (1728–92) was a classical architect. Robert Fergusson (1750–74), born in Edinburgh, was a poet who influenced his more famous countryman, Robert Burns (1759–96), Scotland's greatest lyric poet. The missionary Robert Moffat (1795–1883) served in South Africa, and translated the Bible and Bunyan's *Pilgrim's Progress* into Sechwana. A number of surnames evolved from Robert: Roberts, Robertson, Robson, Robinson, Robeson, Hobson, Hobbes, Hopkin, Hopkins, Dobb and Dobson. Feminine forms are Roberta, Robina, Roby, Robbin, Robena, Robina and Robertina, the last not now favoured. Rupert is a German form of Robert, and ROBIN is fashionable in Scotland. The Gaelic form is *Raibeart*.

ROBIN (m, f) An old and highly favoured pet name for ROBERT which came to be used independently. The legendary Robin Hood is first mentioned by John Fordun (1330–90), the Scottish historian, and until well after the Reformation plays were enacted in Scottish burghs with Robin Hood and Little John the central characters. Town councils like the one in Aberdeen frowned upon these and they were eventually abolished. Many ballads about Robin Hood survive and are mainly of English provenance. Verses on 'Auld Robin Gray' were written to an old Scots tune in 1772 by Lady Anne Lindsay. The parents of Robert Burns seem to have used the pet form for him. A few days after his birth, 25 January 1759, a storm blew down the gable of their cottage at Alloway, and his first welcome to the world was a rough one, as he himself wrote: 'A blast o' Janwar' win, Blew hansel in on Robin'. The name has been used for girls, but Robyn and Robynne are now the favoured forms.

ROBINA (f) A feminine form of ROBERT and ROBIN. An early example is Robina, sister of the Protector, Oliver Cromwell (1599–1658). Robina, daughter of James Lockhart of Cleghorn, who died in 1703, had a daughter also called Robina. Robina Pollok of Pollok (1737–1820) married Hew Crawford of Jordanhill in 1753.

ROBYN (f) A modern feminine form of Robin. It has risen rapidly to popularity in recent years, and is within the top sixty girls' names registered annually. Robyn Morwenna, born 1952, eldest daughter of David

M. Gordon, an Australian of Scottish descent, had a valuable plant named in her honour, *Grevillea Robyn Gordon*. It was named as Australian Plant of the Year in 1984. This may influence use of the name in Australia.

RODERICK (m) Gael. *ruadh-ri* 'red king', and equivalent to the O.G. *Hrodic*, 'famed ruler'. Roderc or Rhydderch, a sixth-century king of Strathclyde, son of Tuathel and an Irish lady, Ethni, received the name from his maternal ancestors. The name was well used in the Gaelic part of Scotland by the MacLeods, MacKenzies and other clans, and from a diminutive form, Rodie or Roddie, evolved the surname of Roddie. John Rhoddie was tidesman at Garlieston in 1792. Roddie is also a common Irish family name from *O'Rodaigh*. The novel, *Roderick Random*, was the first important work of Tobias Smollet (1721–71), and tells the story of a selfish young scape-grace in search of fortune. Sir Walter Scott, in his poem 'The Lady of the Lake', features Roderick Dhu as an outlaw. He also wrote 'The Vision of Don Roderick'. Pet forms of the name are Rod, Rody, Roddy and Rory, the last now used independently as a forename. The Gaelic form is *Ruairidh*, from which evolved MacRuairidh, and the English rendering of Rorieson, which can be abbreviated to Rorie or Rory.

ROGER (m) O.G. compound *hrothi-ger*, meaning 'fame' and 'spear'. The O.E. equivalent gives us *Hrothgar*, and the Normans brought the name to England as Roger. It soon spread to Scotland. Roger of Whitby became Bishop of Orkney before 1109. Roger de Beaumont, son of Robert, Earl of Leicester, and a cousin of King William the Lion, was consecrated Bishop of St Andrews in 1198. Roger, a canon of Abernethy, became Bishop of Ross in 1325. The name was common in the early generations of the Comyns of Buchan in the twelfth century. Roger Hog (1635–1700) of Harcarse, Berwickshire, was a Senator of the College of Justice and ancestor of the Hogs of Newliston, West Lothian, the last of whom, also Roger, died in 1979. The name is also used as a surname, along with Rodger, and another old variant is Hodge. It was usual for pirates on the high seas to fly the 'Jolly Roger', a black flag with crossed white bones and a skull.

ROGNVALD (m) A Norwegian personal name, equivalent to the Gaelic RANALD, RONALD and REGINALD. It was favoured by Kali Kolson, whose mother was Gunhild, sister of Earl Magnus of Orkney. He was Earl himself from before 1139, and shared Caithness with Harald Maddadson. Rognvald was slain in 1139. The name has been sparingly used in Scotland. It is the middle name of Sir Malcolm Rognvald Innes of Edingight, the former Lord Lyon King of Arms, who retired in 2003.

ROLAND (m) O.G. *Hrodland*, probably meaning 'land famous'. The nephew of Charlemange, brave and loyal, was Roland, who has been the hero of numerous romances, including Theroulde's *Chanson de Roland*. It was a favoured name in the Middle Ages, and led to surnames such as Rowland and Rolland. Roland, son of Huchtred, Lord of Galloway, led a force against Donald MacWilliam in the north in 1187. Roland de Carrick, grandson of Duncan, Earl of Carrick, obtained from his grandfather before 1256 a charter granting to him and his heirs the headship of the whole clan. The name has been in regular use, but is not prolific.

RONALD (m) *See* REGINALD.

RONAN (m) Irish Gael, from *ron*, 'sea calf' or 'little seal'. There were several saints so named. Ronan, Abbot of Kingarth, in Bute, died in 737. It is probably from him that *Cill Ronain*, in Islay, and in Kilmarnock, Dumbartonshire are derived. The name has been well used in Ireland and in recent years has become popular in Scotland. See also RHONA.

RORY (m) *See* RODERICK

ROSE (f) O.G. *hros*, 'work horse', but when the Normans brought the name to Britain in the form of *Roese* or *Rhoese*, it was thought to be a flower name. It has been in constant use since then and has given rise to Rosamund and Rosamond, and to compound names such as Rosanna and Roseabella. Rosa is the Latin form, and Rosie is a favourite pet name. Rose appears as a surname of antiquity but in Scotland may be derived from Ross. Rosie is sometimes used independently and with Rosey has been used as a surname since the seventeenth century. In Scott's *Waverley*, Rose is the only child of the Baron of Bradwardine.

ROSALIND (f) Opinions vary as to the origin of this name. Like ROSALINE which may be a variant, it possibly derives from the O.G. compound *hroth*, 'fame', and *lind*, 'shield'. Rosalindis was taken to Spain by the

Goths, where it became Rosalinda. The use of Rosalind in comparatively modern times probably springs from a character so named in *As You Like It*. Edmund Spenser (1552–99) caused confusion by stating in *Shepherd's Calendar* that the name was an anagram of Rosa Daniel. He may not have been aware of the German roots. Rosalinde and Rosalynd are variants.

ROSALINE (f) Probably a variant of the O.G. ROSALIND. It has been much used since the 1840s. Variants are Rosalin, Rosalyn, Roselin and Rozlyn. Roslyn is currently favoured.

ROSAMOND, ROSAMUND (f) The name was brought to Britain by the Normans, and Rosamund is the earlier form. It possibly derives from O.G. *hros*, 'horse', and *munda*, 'protection', but has been associated with the Latin Rosa, meaning 'pure rose'. The name has not been greatly favoured since the Second World War.

ROSINA (f) The Italian diminutive of ROSE and Rosa, and favoured in Scotland. Rosina, daughter of Sir William Purves of Abbeyhill, Edinburgh (1623–84), married James Deans of Woodhouselee, advocate. Rosena is a variant and Rosaleen is fashionable in Ireland.

ROSEMARY (f) Considered to be a borrowed plant name, derived from the Latin *ros*, 'dew' and *marinus*, 'of the sea', thus *rosemarine*, or 'dew of the sea'. A combination of Rose and MARY seems unlikely. The name appears to date from 1745, but came into greater use in the twentieth century.

ROSS (m) A Scottish place-name, from 'cape' or 'headland', which resulted in a prolific surname in the north. The name, however, was first borne by Ayrshire people who came from Yorkshire. Godfrey de Ros, a vassal of Richard de Moreville, obtained the lands of Stewarton in the twelfth century. They were of an entirely different origin, and possibly derived the name from Middle English *rous*, 'red-haired'. Alexander Ross of Balnagown, Master William Ross and William Ross, were among those killed in the Battle of Aldecharwis in 1486. Ross has been used as a forename since the 1840s, and may be due in part to Sir John Ross (1777–1856), the Arctic explorer involved in the search for a 'north-west passage', and to Sir James Clark Ross (1800–62), who also took part in Arctic exploration. The name is now within the top ten most favoured names for boys in Scotland.

ROWENA (f) Derived from the Welsh *Rhonwen*, 'slender fair'. The name may have originated with Godfrey of Monmouth, who gives it to the daughter of Hengist, with whom Vortigern fell in love. In Scott's *Ivanhoe*, Rowena is the Lady of Hargottstandstede, Cedric's ward. She 'drew her descent from Arthur', and Cedric hoped to 'forward the restoration of Saxon independence' by her union with Athelstane. Rowena was naturally mild and gentle.

ROY (m) Gael. *ruadh*, 'red'. The Gaels used it frequently as an epithet, and it appears both as forename and surname. In 1428, Donald Ruffus (i.e. red), had a remission by James I. Hugh, 12th Lord Lovat, was called 'Husten Roy', from the colour of his hair.

The famous freebooter, Rob Roy MacGregor, alias Campbell (1671–1734), is well known in history and legend, and there is a film about him starring Liam Neeson.

RUAIRIDH (m) Gaelic form of RODERICK.

RUTH (f) Of doubtful etymology, but possibly Heb. meaning 'vision of beauty'. The biblical Ruth was a Moabite and the ancestress of the royal line of David. She first married Mahlon, son of Elimelech and NAOMI. Later she befriended a kinsman, Boaz, son of Salmon, who purchased the inheritance of Mahlon and his brother Chilion, and with it Ruth, whom he married. Their son Obel was the father of Jesse, and grandfather of DAVID (OT, Ruth 4:10). Ruth became a popular Christian name soon after the Reformation, and it was favoured by eighteenth-century poets including William Wordsworth (1770–1850) and Mrs F.D. Hemens (1793–835). Some fanciful variants have been recorded, including Ruthalma, Ruthetta and Ruthina. The most common Scottish diminutive, especially in the north-east, is Ruthie.

RYAN (m) An Irish name which has become one of the most popular boys' names in Scotland. The Irish O'Ryans derived their tribe from Drona, fourth in descent from Cahirmore, monarch of Ireland, AD 120–23. The Barony of Idrone, in Carlow, perpetuates the memory of the family. It is probable that the rise to favour of Ryan as a forename is due to the American actor, Ryan O'Neal, who has appeared in *Love Story* and other films.

S

SABINA (f) Lat., 'Sabine woman', from the people of Central Italy, who were united with the Romans. There was a masculine name *Sabinus*, which became obsolete, and two early saints bore the name. It has been in continuous but not wide use since the seventeenth century. Sabine (sometimes called Martha), a daughter of Sgt Maj. David Colyear alias Robertson, of 'Drummond's Regiment', and his wife Jean Bruce, married before 1667, Sir John Nicolson of Tillicoultry. A pet form is Bina, which has been used independently.

SAM (m) Abbreviation of SAMUEL. A 'Sam Browne' was an officer's belt and straps in the First World War, named after General Sir S.J. Browne. In the USA 'Uncle Sam' is the Government, or a typical citizen.

SAMANTHA (f) The name is not well documented, and has been used in Britain only in the last forty years. It was known in the southern states of America in the seventeenth century, and used by white and coloured families. Variants include Samella, Samuela, Samaria and Samentha. It is possibly an Aramaic word for 'listener', but more probably a feminine form of SAMUEL. The use in Scotland seems to have commenced after the screening of *High Society* (1956), in which the late Grace Kelly (who became Princess Grace of Monaco) appeared as Tracy Samantha Lord. More recent use of the name has been influenced by model Samantha Fox,

and it is now within the twenty most favoured girls'
names in Scotland.

SAMUEL (m) Heb., 'heard by God'. Eikanah of Mt Ephriam
had children by his wife Peninnah, but none by his second wife HANNAH; after praying with a priest, she had
a child, Samuel (OT, Samuel 1:2,11,20). He was the
last of the judges of Israel, and inaugurated its first two
kings, Saul and DAVID. The name was rare in Scotland
before the Reformation, but became more popular in
Covenanting times, probably through 'Godly' Samuel
Rutherford (1600–61), minister of Anwoth parish, who
wrote several religious tracts. In Scotland and Ireland
for a considerable period the Gaels used the name to
transliterate *Somhairle* (SOMERLED). Among those who
have lent fame to the name are Samuel Colville, who
resided at St Andrews and wrote an essay on the papacy,
titled *The Grand Imposter Discovered* (1673); Samuel
Clark, Jr. (1769–1814), a Dumfries lawyer who was a
friend of the poet Burns; and Samuel Houston (1793–
1863), of Scots descent, who commanded the Texans
at San Jacinto in 1836, and defeated the Mexicans to
win independence for Texas. He became president of
the new republic and in 1859 was the first state governor. Of course we must not forget the Scottish novelist,
Samuel Rutherford Crockett (1860–1914), who was
Free Church minister at Penicuik in 1886. The great
English lexicographer Dr Samuel Johnson (1793–1863)
greatly influenced the historical literature of the north
and north-west through his published *Journey to the
Western Isles of Scotland*, with James Boswell, in 1773.

Samuel is also a surname, more prolific in England but recorded in Scotland in the seventeenth century. Diminutives of the forename are Sam, Sammie and Sammy, and SAMANTHA is probably a feminine form.

SANDRA (f) *See* ALEXANDRA.

SANDY (m) A favourite Scottish pet name for ALEXANDER.

SARA, SARAH (f) Heb. 'princess'. Sarai, later called Sarah, was the wife of Abram, later called ABRAHAM. She was barren, but in later life, supposedly by divine intervention, bore him a son, ISAAC. Sarah died at Kirjatharba, in Canaan (OT, Genesis 13:16). Another Sarah, sole surviving kin of Raguel, married Tobias, son of Tobit (a Jewish captive in Ninevah), after seven previous marriages had been wrecked by the evil spirit Asmodus. In Gaelic Sarah is equivalent to Mòrag, earlier rendered Mor or More. The *Old Parochial Register of Dunoon & Kilmun* has the following entry:

> 1787: *Born the 1st and baptized the 3rd, both days of Jan[ua]ry, Janet, d[aughte]r lawful to James Clark and More McPhorich, alias Sarah Lamont, spouses in Kilbride in this parish.*

Variants are Sara, Saraid and Sairi, and the name is often linked with Ann, Jane or Jayne, and Louise. The pet names Sally and Sadie are still used in Scotland. See also ZARA.

SCOTT (m) An old surname, now much used as a forename. The surname was common along both sides of the Scotland-England border in the twelfth century.

The first on record bore an English forename – Uchtred *filius* Scott – and witnessed an inquisition of Earl David about 1124. The name became prolific in Northumberland. Many landed families in the Border counties of Scotland have borne the surname, enshrined forever in the fame of Sir Walter Scott. As a forename, Scott has been much used since the time of novelist Scott Fitzgerald (Francis Scott Key Fitzgerald, 1895–1940), and is now in the top five favourite names for boys. Scot is not often used.

SEAN (m) *See* SHAUN.

SEBASTIAN (m) Lat. *Sebastianus*, 'man of Sebastia', a city of Pontus, derived from a Greek word meaning 'venerable'. St Sebastian was a Roman legionary martyred under Diocletian. Because he was bound to a tree and shot at with arrows, he is patron saint of archers and soldiers, also of pin-makers. The name appears to have come into Cornwall from Spain, and later into Scotland, where it has been used sparingly. In Scott's novel *The Abbot*, Sebastian is a favoured servant of Queen Mary, and married one of her attendants. Its modern use has probably been influenced by the famous English athlete, Sebastian Coe (now Lord Coe), who broke twelve world track records.

SELINA (f) The origin of this name is obscure, and it has often been confused with DIANA. It may derive phonetically from the Latin Coelina, from *caelum*, 'heaven', through the French form Céline, Salén. The name has not been widely used in Scotland. Catherine Selina, born 1800, daughter of Archibald Hamilton Cathcart

(4th son of Charles, 9th Lord Cathcart), married in 1839, Robert Smith of Capenhurst House, Chester. TV personality Selina Scott was educated at Aberdeen.

SELVACH (m, f) Gael., 'rich in possessions'. This is the phonetic spelling of *Selbhach*, and was originally used for men. In 736, Aengus, son of Fergus, King of the Picts, wasted Dalriada, and bound in chains two sons of its late king, Selbhach, usually called Eachach. The name came to be used for women. In Ivory Burnett's novel *The Ravens Enter the House* (1931), Selvach is foster-sister and nurse to Catherine Cameron, the young wife of Neil Campbell of Glenlonan.

SENGA (f) An artificial, but attractive name formed by the letters of AGNES reversed.

SETON (m) The name appears as a surname about 1146, when Alexander Seton witnessed a charter by David I. The family appear to have originated in Flanders, and the surname derives from Sai, near Exmes. The use as a forename probably dates from the nineteenth century. Seton Gordon (1886–1976) the naturalist and author was a native of Aberdeen.

SEUMAS (m) Irish Gael. form of JAMES. Scott, in his novel, *Waverley*, has Shemus an Snachad, 'James of the needle', as the tailor to Vich Ian Vohr; also Shemus Beg ('little'), a blind harper who visited Donald Bean Lean.

SHANNON (m, f) Gael. *Seandun*, 'old fort'. From a place-name and river in County Cavan, Ireland, also used as a surname in that country. It appeared as a forename in the 1930s and has mainly been used for girls. Twenty-five were registered in Scotland in 1990. Its rise may be due to the character so named in TV's *Beverley Hills*, and more recently to Shannon, in the Australian 'soap opera' *Home and Away*.

SHARON (m, f) Heb., 'the plain'. Derived from a plain lying between Jaffa and Mount Carmel. There is a reference to 'Sharon's dewy rose', in Hymn 309, in *The Church Hymnary*, and to 'the rose of Sharon', a beautiful shepherdess, in the *Song of Songs*, but Sharon did not become a personal name in biblical times. It was adopted as a Christian name by the Puritans and carried to America, where it was known also as a male name. A British bearer of the name was the lawyer and historian, Sharon Turner (1768–1847). 'Rose of Sharon' became Rosasharn in Steinbecks' *Grapes of Wrath* (1939), later a film. Other recorded variants are Sharan, Sharane, Sharene, Sharone and Sharonne. It is becoming a popular female name in Scotland. Pet forms are Shari, Sharie and Shara. Sharonda occurs in the USA.

SHAUN (m) A phonetic form of the Irish SEAN, derived from JOHN through the French Jean. The English style is Shane, boosted by the classic western film of that name (1953), which starred Alan Ladd (1913–64). Shane has occasionally been used for girls: a phonetic rendering of the Welsh Sian, meaning JANE. Probably the most famous Sean of modern times is the Scots film star, Sir Sean Connery.

SHEILA (f) A phonetic form of the Irish Sine, itself derived from Celia (CECILIA). It became popular in the 1930s and is still in use. Variants are Shiela, Sheelagh, Sheelah, Shelia and Shelah. The favoured Gaelic form is Shelagh. Sheila is an Australian slang name for young women, but is said to derive from *shaler*, 'sheller'.

SHONA (f) *See* SINEAD.

SIBYL (f) *See* CYBIL. In Scott's *Kenilworth*, Sibyl Laneham is Master Robert's wife. She had 'played the devil ere now, in a Mystery in Queen Mary's time'.

SILVESTER, SYLVESTER (m) Lat. *silva*, 'belonging to a wood'. The name has been used since early Christian times, and was adopted by three popes. It came to Scotland in the late twelfth century, and has been used as a surname. An early instance of its use as a Christian name is in 1463, when Silvester Rattray of Craighall, Perthshire, was an ambassador extraordinary to the English court. The name appears in later generations of that family. An emigrant from Loch Awe, Argyll, to Ontario, Canada, in 1824 was Sylvester Campbell.

SILVIA (f) Lat. *silvius*, 'of the wood'. Rhea Silvia was the mother of Romulus and Remus, the founders of Rome. Silvia came into use as a forename in Italy at the Renaissance, and, like some other classical names, it came to England in Elizabethan times. Shakespeare has Silvia as a noblewoman in his *Two Gentlemen of Verona* (1594), and the play includes the famous song 'Who is Silvia?'. Other writers have made use of the variant Sylvia, which is now the most favoured spelling in Scotland. Sylvie is a pet form.

SIMON (m) Heb. 'listening'. Simon, akin to Simeon, is a common name in the scriptures (OT, and NT). Simon, who was given the name PETER, is the most important, being the legendary founder of the Christian Church in Rome. His name was popular throughout Europe in the Middle Ages, but like PETER, it went out of favour after the Reformation because of the Catholic associations. However, the Catholic Frasers of Lovat kept the name before the public, and there was a revival in the present century. Possibly Simon Templar, 'the Saint', in the novels of Leslie Charteris, gave some impetus. The Gaels simply render the name Sim or Simon, and surnames which have evolved include Sim, Simson, Simm, Simpson and Symson. Some of these forms appear also as forenames. Simonne has been used as a feminine form, but the French Simone is more popular in Scotland. Simon Gray, a retired London businessman residing in Duns, considered himself a poet and gave Robert Burns a sight of his work when the bard was on his Border tour. The views of the traveller were scathing! Simon Glendinning, of an ancient race (Glendonwyne), appears in Scott's novel, *The Monastery*.

SIMONE (f) *See* SIMON.

SINE (f) A Gaelic form JANE or JEAN.

SINEAD (f) An Irish form of JANET, in current use in Scotland, and rendered Seonid by the Gaels. In England SHONA is the equivalent.

SIOBHAN (f) Gael. A rendering of JUDITH which appears also as Siubhan, Shavon, Shavonne, Shervan and Shevonne. The phonetic mode is *Sh'vaun*. In Ireland it is often an anglicised form of Susan, and JUDITH can be synonymous with JULIE. Siobhan McKenna (1923–86) was a famous Irish actress. Today actress Siobhan Redmond appears in many TV productions.

SOMERLED (m) O.Nor. *Sumarlith*, 'summer wanderer'. An ancient and historic name in the West Highlands and in the Hebrides. Somerled 'the mighty' was ruler or *regulus* of the Isles, and married Ragnhild, daughter of Olaf, King of Man and the Isles. From him descended the MacDonalds and the MacDougals. The MacDonalds and the MacMillans favoured the name Somerled, often rendered *Somhairle* (*see* also SORLEY). In many cases it has given way to Samuel.

SONIA (f) A Russian diminutive of SOPHIA, rendered Sonja in Scandinavia and popularised by the Olympic figure skater, Sonja Henie (1912–69), who starred in ten films. It came into Britain at the beginning of the present century, and may have been partly influenced by Stephen McKenna's novel *Sonia* (1917). The variant Sonya is also used in Scotland.

SOPHIA (f) Gr., 'wisdom'. The name was favoured in the Eastern Church on account of a mosque at Constantinople named St Sophia's. It spread into Central Europe, then into England, and was used by royals. King James VI and Anna of Denmark had a daughter Sophia born at Greenwich in 1606, but she died in infancy. The mother and wife of George I, who became king in 1714, were both named Sophia. The name was common in Scotland in the early seventeenth century. Sophia, daughter of Alexander Seton, Earl of

Dunfermline, by his first wife Lilias Drummond, married 1611/12, David, 1st Lord of Lindsay of Balcarres. Sophia, daughter of Francis, Earl of Errol, married Lord John Gordon, created Viscount Melgum and Lord Aboyne in 1627, and died in 1642. The name is now within the seventy most popular names in Scotland, and it seems possible the Italian actress Sophia Loren, born 1934, star of *Two Women* (1969, Academy Award) has influenced its use. Sophie is the most popular form in Scotland, and Phie (pronounced Fye) is a pet name.

SORLEY (m) A late form of SOMERLED, also used as a surname. MacSorley is recorded in the fourteenth century, also Sorleyson. Sorley MacLean, born on the island of Raasay, was a notable poet.

STACEY (m, f) This now popular name was originally a male surname recorded as Staci in England as early as 1270. However its use as a forename stems from Anastasia, Greek root, 'resurrection'. Anastasia was fashionable in England in the thirteenth century, usually abbreviated to Anstey or Anstice. It has always been popular in Russia, and the 1956 film *Anastasia*, in which the late Ingrid Bergman starred as the daughter of the last Czar, kept the name fresh and interesting. Stacy Keach, born 1941, the American actor, has won awards for stage work and appeared in several films. Feminine forms in current use in Scotland are Stacey, Stacie and Stacy; the first highly favoured.

STEPHANIE (f) Feminine form of the French Stephan (STEPHEN), also appearing in Scotland as Steffani and Steffanie. Stephana and Stephania have been found elsewhere. It is possible that the popular American actress Stephanie Powers has had some influence on use of the name. Fanny is occasionally used as a pet name. The diminutives Steffi, Stevi and Stevie are often used independently.

STEPHEN (m) Gr. *Stephanos*, from a word meaning 'crown' or garland'. The laurel wreath was the highest honour a man could attain in the classical world. Stephen, who was 'full of faith and power', was the first Christian martyr stoned to death (NT, Acts 6:8; 8:59–60). According to legend his body was recovered by Gamaliel. The name was popular in early Christian times and came to England after the Conquest. It gave rise to surnames which include Stephen, Stephens, Steven, Stevens, Stevenson and Stein. In Scotland, Sir Stephen Lockhart of Cleghorn had a charter of his lands in 1476. Thomas Steuen rented land in Auchinarn, near Glasgow, in 1509. The Gaelic form of Stephen is *Steaphan*, and in Wales Steffan is the usual spelling. STEPHANIE is the feminine form. Stephen Clarke (died 1797) was an Edinburgh musician brought in by James Johnson to harmonise the airs for his *Scots Musical Museum* to which Robert Burns contributed. Scott has 'a magnificent-looking man', Stephanos, a wrestler, in *Count Robert of Paris*. Count Stephen appears in his novel, *Ivanhoe*. The best-known bearer of the name in Scotland at this time is Stephen Hendry, the wealthy seven-times world snooker champion.

STEVEN (m) *See* STEPHEN.

STEWART (m) O.S. *sti weard*, the person who looked after

the domestic animals in a large medieval establishment. By an extension of meaning, it came to be used in relation to one who provided for his master's table. By the eleventh century the word had come to mean one who supervised the household affairs of another. In Scotland, the steward was chief of the royal household, and his duties extended to the collection and management of the revenues. The chevron chequy seen in the heraldry of the family and of those who came to be associated with them, is said to represent an ancient method of keeping accounts. The earliest mention of steward with the final letter changed to 't' is in the late fourteenth-century *Armorial de Gelre*. The Royal House of Steward descended from the stewards. The variant STUART is recorded in the fourteenth century, and stabilised after the residence in France of Mary, Queen of Scots. Steuart is another form of the name. The Gaels render the name *Stiubhart*. Stupert is an old Ayrshire name, but it seems likely that in some cases the surname Stupart derives from the Gaelic form. Stewart and Stuart have been used as forenames since the second half of the nineteenth century and the latter spelling is much favoured. Steuart has also been in use, but very seldom. The portrait of Steuart Bayley Hog (1864–1944), of Newliston and Kellie, was painted by Ernest Stephen Lumsden (1883–1948).

STRUAN (m) Derived from Strowan, a parish in Perthshire linked with Monzievaird, and from the estate of Strowan, long the home of the Robertson chiefs. It was often called Struan. Capt. Alasdair Stewart Robertson

(1863–1910) was called 'Struan' Robertson, and the name – still in use – is borne mainly by Robertsons.

STUART (m) *See* STEWART.

SUIBHNE (m) This old name is of uncertain origin. Dr G.F. Black says it has nothing to do with the O.Nor. *Sveinn* (SWAIN), but is the root of the Irish Sweeney. Dr W.J. Watson, however, says the name is preserved in *Caistael Suibhne*, Castle Sween in Knapdale. The earliest reference to the name is in the *Annals of Ulster*, which record in 1034 the death of Suibhne mac Cinaeda ri Gallgaidhel, 'Suibhne, son of Kenneth, king of Gallgaidil'. Some MacQueens are believed to have been MacSuibhnes. Suibhne MacDonald, who emigrated to Waterloo County, Ontario, Canada, before 1836 and died *c.* 1863, was known as 'Sweden' MacDonald.

SUSAN (f) *See* SUSANNA.

SUSANNA (f) Heb *Shushannah*, 'lily'. The saint who saves from infamy and reproach. This from her fiery trial recorded in the tale of Susannah and the Elders. In *The Apocrypha*, Susannah is the wife of Joiachim, accused of adultery and condemned to death by the Jewish elders, but DANIEL stood up for her and proved her innocence. Another Susanna (NT, Luke 8:3) was among the women who ministered to Jesus as he went about preaching. The name is sometimes found in the Middle Ages, but did not become prolific until the seventeenth century. Old forms of the name are Susanney and Shusanna. Susanna MacIver was the author of *Cookery and Pastry* (1787), in which she gives a recipe for haggis, in those days a luxury dish. Susan is a short form. Susan Logan, sister of 'thairm-inspiring rattlin' Willie [Major Logan]', was sent a poem by Burns, with Beattie's *Poems*, as a New Year gift, January 1787. The name is rendered *Siùsan* in Gaelic. Variants currently in use in Scotland are Susanna, Susannah, Susanne, Suzannah and Suzanne, the last being the most popular. Short forms are Sue, Sukey and Suzy.

SUZANNE (f) *See* SUSANNA.

SWAIN (m) O.Nor. *Sveinn*, 'a boy'. The name was also used in Middle English. Swein, 'Ulfkills sune', is a witness to King Edgar's charter granting Swinton to the Monks of St Cuthbert at Coldingham, *c.* 1100. Swein, son of Thor, ancestor of the Earls of Gowrie, who adopted the territorial surname of Ruthven, settled in Perthshire early in the reign of David I (1124–53). King Swein of Denmark had three sons, and aided Edger Aetheling in an attack on York in 1069. The name appears throughout the Middle Ages in forms such as Swane, Swayne and Sweyne, and appears as a surname from the thirteenth century. Elyas Sweyn, constable at Leuchars, Fife, appears as a witness in two charters, *c.* 1250. Other surnames which have evolved are Swan, Swann, Swanney and MacSwan. Use as a forename continued. James Grant, VIIth of Freuchie, had a natural daughter who married Sweyne Grant of Ballintomb, who died in 1633. *See also* SUIBHNE.

SYBIL (f) *See* SIBYL.

T

TABITHA (f) Aramaic, 'roe', or 'gazelle', equivalent to the Gr. *Dorcas*. The biblical Tabitha (NT, Acts 9:36) was a woman 'full of good works', who died and was raised from the dead by PETER. The scene is depicted in the Brancacci chapel in St Maria del Carmine, Florence, executed by Massaccio. The name went out of favour in Britain early in the present century, but reappeared in the 1960s. Although not prolific, the name is in current use in Scotland.

TAM (m) A Scottish short form or pet name for THOMAS, sometimes used independently, as in the case of Tam Dalyell, the Labour MP for Linlithgow. A 'Tam o' Shanter' is a round bonnet, from the name of the famous poem of the name by Robert Burns.

TAMAR (f) Heb., meaning 'date palm'. The biblical Tamar was a daughter of DAVID and passionately desired by her half-brother, Amnon, who raped her, but came to dislike her. She was avenged by her full brother, Absolom, who had him killed two years later (OT, 2 Samuel 13:11–15, 28–9). The name occurs in Russian literature, but did not come into use in Britain until the sixteenth century. Recorded variants are Tamah, Tamer, Tamor, Tamour, Tayma and Thamer. It has been overtaken to some extent by the Russian form TAMARA, and fifteen girls of the name were registered in Scotland in 1990. In America, this is a popular name among coloured people, including actress Tamara Dobson.

TANYA (f) Derived from Tatiana a martyr who suffered AD 225, and is venerated in the Orthodox Church. The name is very popular in Russia, sometimes as the original Tatiana, or as Tanya and Tonya. Tatianus was a masculine form and the name of several saints. Tania and Tanya are currently in use in Scotland.

TARA (f) Derived from the Irish Gaelic word for 'hill'. There are a number of places there called Tara: one in County Meath with royal associations. The poet Thomas Moore (1779–1852) highlighted the name in his *Irish Melodies* (1814). The modern use of the name is due to TV films made since about the commencement of the Second World War, and probably a further boost was given when the actor Anthony Newly and his former wife, actress Joan Collins, named a daughter Tara in 1963.

TERENCE (m) Lat. *Terentius*, the name of a Roman *gens* of obscure etymology. There was a third-century saint called Terentius, and the name came into frequent use in Ireland, where it is used for the native Turlough. It has made it way to Scotland where it is in current, but quiet use. Terrence is a variant and Terry is a favourite diminutive.

THEODORA (f) Feminine form of THEODORE, sometimes resulting in the pet form DORA, which it shares with DOROTHEA.

THEODORE (m) Gr., meaning 'gift of God'. The name

appears on early Christian monuments and seems to have evolved separately from Theophilis (Gr., 'friend of God'). The name was borne by several saints, one of whom instituted the parish system in England. Theodore, 'King of Corsica', was otherwise known as Baron Theodore de Neuhoff (1686–1756), and was successively in French, Swedish and Spanish service. Theodore Gordon (1789–1870) served his apprenticeship as a watchmaker in Aberdeen and went to London, where he made horizontal and duplex escapements. He was for a time editor of the *Horological Magazine*. The name has been used in Scotland since the seventeenth century. The greater use of it in America is doubtless due to Theodore Roosevelt, President 1901–9. Pet forms of the name are Theo, Ted and Teddy. The feminine form is THEODORA.

TERESA, THERESA (f) Said to be derived from the Gr. word for 'reap', but in fact the origin of the name is obscure. It is rendered *Theresia* in Latin, but Teresa is common in Italy. One of the earliest references is in the fifth century when Thereasia appears as wife of St Paulinus, Bishop of Nola, but she was of Spanish extraction. The name became better known through St Teresa of Avila (1515–82), and in Britain the name became favoured through St Therese of Lisieux (1873–97), especially by Roman Catholic families. TRACEY is sometimes equivalent. Tess and Tessa are pet names. In *The Antiquary*, Scott has Teresa D'Acunha as a Spanish servant of the Countess of Glenallan.

THOMAS (m) Aramaic, meaning 'twin'. In the scriptures

it is the name of one of the apostles, also known as
'Didymus', Gr. for a twin. His real name may have been
Judah, and he may have been called 'Didymus' to dis-
tinguish him from two other Judahs. Thomas was not
present when Jesus appeared before the apostles after the
resurrection, and he refused to believe it, hence the term
'doubting Thomas'. Christ later appeared to him and
showed his wounds, which convinced him. The name
was borne by a few ecclesiastics in England before the
Norman Conquest, and it came more into use. Thomas
of Bayeux, Bishop of York died in 1100. In Scotland,
Magister Thomas witnessed a grant to the canons of
Holyrood in 1128. Thomas, son of Cospatrick, and
brother of Alan, appears on record in 1151. Thomas
Learmonth, otherwise called 'Thomas the Rymer', a
native of Ercildoune, lived in the reign of Alexander III
(1249–86) and was famous for his predictions. In 1294,
Thomas de Kirkcudbright was consecrated Bishop of
Galloway, and he became chaplain to King Robert I.
The name was in use throughout the later Middle Ages
and also appeared as a surname, giving rise to names
such as Thom, Thomson, Thompson, Tomison and
Thomsone. Four generations of gunsmiths at Doune
between 1646 and 1800 were named Thomas Caddell.
Thomas Ruddiman (1674–1757), sometime Keeper of
the Advocate's Library in Edinburgh, was an eminent
Latinist, and his *Rudiments of the Latin Tongue* was
a classic textbook for generations of scholars. Other
famous Scots who have borne the name include Thomas
Campbell (1774–1844), a popular poet in his time,
and Thomas Carlyle (1795–1881), an eminent man of

letters. Short forms of the name are TAM, Tammy, Tom and Tommie or Tommy. The Gaelic form is *Tamhus* or *Tomas*, and the old feminine form is THOMASINA.

THOMASINA (f) Feminine form of THOMAS. Tamsin is also an early form, probably of Cornish origin, and still in use. Other forms in current use in Scotland are Tammie and Tammy. Sina is an occasional pet name.

TIMOTHY (m) Gr., *Timotheos*, 'honoured of God'. The biblical Timothy was a convert and companion of PAUL, and was co-author or amanuensis of a number of his letters (NT, Romans 16:21). It was a fairly common name among early Christians and came into use in Britain after the Reformation. It is in current but not wide use in Scotland, and some surnames such as Tims and Timms have emerged. Tim and Timmy are diminutives.

TORMOD (m) *See* NORMAN.

TORQUIL (m) O.Nor. *Thork[et]ill*, possibly meaning 'Thor's cauldron'. In Gaelic it became *Torcail*, whence Torquil. Torquil, son of Leod, held part of the island of Lewis at the close of the thirteenth century. His descendants became known as the *Siol Torcuil*. Torquil continued as a forename among the MacLeods, but appears also in England, where it was probably introduced by the Danes in the thirteenth century, and gave rise to a number of surnames, including Thurkettle, Thurkle and Thirkell.

TRACY, TRACEY (m, f) A Norman place-name which came to be used as both forename and surname. For a time, mainly in the nineteenth century, it was used as a Christian name for boys, but it is now wholly feminine. Sometimes it is a variant of THERESA. The name gained prominence after the screening of the film *High Society* (1956) in which Grace Kelly's character was Tracy Samantha Lord. The forms Tracy, Tracey and Tracie are all in current use in Scotland.

U

UCHTRED (m) O.E. 'sprite counsel'. A very old personal name which survived the Norman Conquest. It is recorded in various forms – Huchtred, Vhtred, Utred, Wihtred and Uchtryd. There was a feminine form, Ochtreda or Hughtreda, found in the family of Dunbar of Dunbar, whence it came through Uchtred, Earl of Northumberland. The Dunbars are linked through marriage with the ancient lords of Galloway. Uchtred, son of Fergus, who shared the rule of that district which his brother Gilbert, is on record in 1136. Helias, son of Huchtred, received from Waldeve, son of Gospatrick a charter of the lands of Dundas, near Queensferry, about the middle of the twelfth century. The descendants took the name Dundas as their surname, but did not continue the name Huchtred.

UNA (f) *See* OONAGH.

URSULA (f) Lat., from the diminutive *ursa*, the feminine form of *ursus*, 'bear' and originally 'she-bear'. It was the name of a famous saint, martyred through Attila the Hun in the fifth century. Ursula was not a prolific name in the Middle Ages, but occurs in England, Ireland and Scotland in the seventeenth century. It was in frequent use by the families of the Lords Fairfax, and spread as far as the Shetlands Isles. The testament of Ursilla Edmesson, wife of Ninian Neven of Windhouse, Shetland, was confirmed in 1648. Ursula is in current but not wide use.

V

VALENTINE (m, f) Lat. *valens*, the participle of *valeo*, 'strong, healthy'. It is used both as a male and female name, and as a surname. The Roman Emperor Valentinian, who lived 321–57, had sons Gratianus and Valentinian. The Valentines of Fettercairn in Kincardineshre, are said to have sprang from Valentine of Thornton, who lived in the reign of King Robert I (1306–29). The surname appears in records as Wallentyne, Wallentine, Weland, Wiland or Weyland. The latter name appears in the genealogy of the Chisholms, *c.* 1500. As a forename, Valentine is in current use but is not prolific. Val is a pet name.

VALERIE (f) Lat. feminine of *Valerius*, a Roman clan name derived from the same root as Valentine and meaning 'to be strong'. St Valerie was an early saint, and Valerianus was proclaimed Roman emperor by the legions in Rhaetia after the murder of Gallus in 253. Valeria became known in France and was imported into England, where the name was popular in the late nineteenth century. Valerie is in regular use in Scotland. Valery is a variant, and Val is a diminutive, shared with VALENTINE.

VANESSA (f) The name was invented by Jonathan Swift (1667–1745), with reference to Esther Vanhomrigh, who fell in love with him. He tells of the affair in his poem, *Cadenus and Vanessa*; 'cadenus' being an anagram of the Latin *decanus*, meaning 'dean'. It seems to have been simply a literary name before the 1920s. Sir Hugh Walpole (1884–1941) published his novel *Vanessa* in 1933. The actress, Vanessa Redgrave, born 1937, and made a CBE in 1967, has given prominence to the name, which is in current use in Scotland. Nessa and Nessie are pet names.

VERONICA (f) Lat. *vera iconica*, 'true image'. St Veronica is the name traditionally given to the woman who washed Christ's face when he was on the way to Calvary. A 'true image' of his face is said to have appeared on the cloth she used. The name came from the Continent to Scotland. Alexander [Bruce], 2nd Earl of Kincardine, married (contract dated 1659), Veronica Van Arsen, daughter of Baron Corneille Van Somelsdyke, in Holland. She was a great-grandmother of James Boswell (1740–1822), the biographer of Samuel Johnson. Alexander Bruce of Broomhall, Fife, who died in 1715, had a daughter Veronica, who married (as his second wife), Gustav Hamilton, merchant burgess of Edinburgh; secondly, in 1703, Duncan Campbell of Kames. The name is fairly well used today. Vera, Ron and Ronnie are pet names.

VICTOR (m) Lat. *victor*, 'conqueror'. It was a prolific name in the time of the Roman Empire, and the name of an early pope, AD 193. The name was not prolific in the Middle Ages, and came into use in France about the time of the Revolution. In Scotland it was uncommon until the reign of Queen Victoria (1837–1901), when used as a masculine form. Victor Alexander Sereld [Gore] (1876–1928), Lord Kilmarnock, succeeded his father as 21st Earl of Errol in 1927. Vic is the usual pet form of the name.

VICTORIA (f) Lat. 'victor'. The name appears in inscriptions on women's tombs of the Roman Empire period. It was sparingly used in the Middle Ages, but reached Scotland by c. 1600. Victoria, a younger daughter of Archibald, 7th Earl of Argyll, by his second Countess, Anne Cornwallis, was born c. 1616. She became an Augustinian canoness, and in 1687/88 received a pension of £40 yearly from King James VII. The name, however, did not become popular until the reign of Queen Victoria. It is now even more fashionable, and about the twenty-fifth most popular name for girls. Short forms in current use are Vicki, Vickie, Vicky and Vikki, all of which also appear independently.

VINCENT (m) Lat. 'conquering', from the same root as
VICTOR. There was a third-century martyr of this
name at Saragossa, whose cult was extensive. The
name is found in England from the fourteenth century.
Later, the fame of St Vincent Ferrer, a fifteenth century Spanish Dominican friar, helped spread the name.
Moreover, there was St Vincent de Paul, founder in
the seventeenth century of the Vincentian Order of
the Sisters of Charity, and the name became popular
with Roman Catholic families. Vincent also became a
surname. Scott has Vincent Jenkin as a sharp-witted
apprentice in *The Fortunes of Nigel*. The name is in
current, but not wide use, in Scotland. Short forms are
Vince and Vincey.

VIOLET (f) Lat., a flower name derived from the word
Viola, the French diminutive of which was Violette.
The name was used by Shakespeare for his heroine of
Twelfth Night, in the form Viola, a sister of SEBASTIAN.
The name came early to Scotland due to French influence. Violet, daughter of Laurence Middleton of that
Ilk, married secondly, *c.* 1496, George Leslie of that
Ilk, and died before 1505. Robert Dalzell of Glenae,
created Baronet in 1666, had a daughter Violet, daughter of William Douglas of Pumpherston, married
c. 1609, Andrew Riddel of that Ilk. It was a favourite
name among Whytes in Dunoon and Kilmun parish.
Violet Jacob (1863–1946) was an Angus poetess who
wrote songs of the soil and the sea. The colour violet is
said to indicate the love of truth. Vi is a pet name, but
the parent name is not now fashionable.

VIRGIL (m) An English form of *Vergilius*, a Roman clan name, later written *Vergenius*, and made famous by the poet Virgil (Publius Vergilius Maro), born 70 BC. An eighth-century Irish St Virgilius was probably originally Fearghal. The name has never been fashionable in Scotland. See also VIRGINIA.

VIRGINIA (f) Lat. 'maiden'. This was originally a Roman clan name, Vergenius (see VIRGIL). From the fourth century the name came to be spelt Virginia. The modern use of the name dates from 1584, when Sir Walter Raleigh founded the North American colony of Virginia, naming it for Elizabeth Tudor, 'the virgin Queen'. The name has been very popular in America. The first white child born in America of English parentage was Virginia Dare, at Ronoake in 1587. Virginia, born 1773, in the state so named, was a younger daughter of John [Murray], 4th Earl of Dunmore, Governor of New York in 1769, and subsequently of Virginia. The name became more into use in Britain in the nineteenth century. Virginia Wade, the tennis player, author and commentator, winner of many tournaments, including Wimbledon in 1977, has kept the name before the public. Ginny is a diminutive.

VIVIAN (m, f) Lat. *Vivianus*, derived from *vivus*, 'alive' or 'lively'. The name occurs in early Roman records, but has never been prolific. It was occasionally spelt Phythian or Fithian in the Middle Ages. There is a suggestion that some bearers of the name were in fact NINIAN, misread in old documents. Sir Vivian Fuchs, the Antarctic explorer and author, is possibly the best-known modern bearer of the name. Vivian has been used for girls, but the usual form is VIVIEN.

VIVIEN (f) Derived from the French Vivienne. Vivien was a 'wily wanton' in the legendary King Arthur's court, who hated all the knights. She attempted to seduce Arthur and succeeded in compromising Merlin. Tennyson used the name in his poem 'Vivien', part of *The Idylls of the King (1859)*. Vivien Leigh (1913–67), who starred as Scarlett O'Hara, in the blockbuster film, *Gone with the Wind* (1939), changed her Christian name from Vivian. Both Vivien and Vivienne are in current use in Scotland, but outwith the top one hundred girls' names. Vyvian and Vyvyan have been recorded. Viv is a pet name.

W

WALTER (m) O.G., originally *Waldhar* or *Wealdhere*, 'powerful warrior', the name was in Anglo-French *Wautier*. In Latin documents it is usually rendered *Waltero*. Waltero de Bolebec witnessed a charter by David I, King of Scots, to the priory of the Isle of May, *c.* 1150. Walter *dapifero* (steward) witnessed a charter by Robert the Bishop, to the priory of St Andrews *c.* 1153. The name came into use as a surname. Henry Waltere in Innerkethyn is on record in 1391. Other surnames which have evolved from Walter are Walterson, and (from the short forms Wat and Wattie) Watt, Watts, Watson, Watkins and Waters. The Gaelic form of Walter is *Bhaltair*. Walter, High Steward of Scotland, who died in 1177, founded the Abbey of Paisley for the monks of Clugny in 1164. It was a much-favoured name among the Scotts. Walter Scott (1614–94) of Satchells, wrote a doggerel history of the Scotts (1688), and of course the best known is Sir Walter Scott (1771–1832), the great novelist and poet. The popularity of the name has declined in recent years.

WAYNE (m) Derived from the occupation of making waggons – a wainwright. The modern use of the name in Scotland, however, is almost certainly due to the films of the late American actor John Wayne (Marion Michael Morrison).

WENDY (f) The name was first used by the Scots author James M. Barrie (1860–1937). He adapted it from a pet name, 'Friendy-Wendy', given to him as a child by Margaret Henley. There was previously a German feminine name derived from Vanda to become Wanda, meaning 'stock' or 'stem', which might have suggested Wendy. The name came into general use in the early 1920s. Several actresses, including Dame Wendy Hiller, have kept the name before the public. It is in regular use in Scotland, but not prolific.

WILFRED (m) O.E. *will-frid*, 'resolute for peace'. St Wilfrith or Wilfrid (*c.* 634–709), Bishop of York, is recorded by Bede, and many churches were dedicated to him. The name has been sparingly used in Scotland.

WILHELMINA (f) The feminine form of WILLIAM borrowed from the German or Dutch. Recorded variants are Williamina and Willielma. The last was the name of the daughter of Dr William Maxwell of Preston, who married Lord Glenorchy (1738–71), and founded a number of churches including 'Lady Glenorchy's North', later Hillside, in Edinburgh. Wilhelmina Alexander (1756–1843), sister of the Laird of Ballochmyle, was the inspiration for Burns' song, 'The Bonnie Lass of Ballochmyle'. Short forms of the name are Willa, Willie, Mina, Minna, Minnie, Wilma and Willina, and the last two frequently appear independently.

WILLIAM (m) O.G. *vila-helma*, a compound meaning 'helmet of resolution'. It was Latinised Willelmus or Gulielmus, and became Guillaume in French, used both as forename and surname. William the Conqueror brought the name to England. William the Lion, King of Scots (1165–1214), was the son of Earl Henry and grandson of David I and Queen Maud. Many ecclesiastics were named William. The mid-thirteenth century bishops of Argyll and Caithness bore the name, and four clerics named William were bishops of Orkney in the thirteenth and fourteenth centuries. William Wallace fought bravely for Scottish independence, 1270–1305, after the abdication of John Balliol. The part of Wallace in the film *Braveheart*, is played by Mel Gibson. William Dunbar (1460–1513), a Franciscan monk born in East Lothian, whose poetical works were written for the court rather than the common people, was admired by Sir Walter Scott and more recently by the late Hugh MacDiarmid. Many surnames have evolved from William, including Williams, Williamson, Wilson, Wilcox, Wilmot, Wilkins and Willis. The German form Wilhelm is not now popular. In Gaeldom the name is rendered *Uilleam*, and the old feminine form was WILHELMINA. Pet forms of William are Will, Willie, Bill and Billy.

WILMA (f) *See* WILHELMINA.

WINIFRED (f) There has been some confusion regarding this name, either Welsh *Gwenfrewi*, 'friend of peace', or O.E. Winfrith (from which comes the masculine WILFRED), 'win to peace', but most Winifreds rightly favour the Welsh derivation. St Winifred, a seventh-century saint of Welsh birth, was beheaded by Caradoc, a chieftain from Flintshire, for refusing to marry him. She is esteemed as the patron saint of virgins. The name has been in regular use since the sixteenth century, and it was highly favoured from the late Victorian period to the 1930s. Lady Winifred Maxwell Constable (1736–1801) composed an air, 'The Banks of the Cree', for which Burns wrote a song, but the tune is unfortunately lost. Recorded variant spellings are Winefred, Winifride, Winnifred and Wynifred. The Gaelic form is Oonagh (see OONA). Pet names are Freda (seldom used) and Winnie.

WINSTON (m) The name is territorial, derived from a place near Cirencester, in Gloucestershire, probably meaning 'Wine's settlement'. The name – also used as a surname – has been favoured by the Churchill family since 1620, when Sir Winston Churchill, father of

the Duke of Marlborough, was born. His mother was
Sarah Winston. Despite the fame of Britain's famous
Second World War (1939–45) Prime Minister and historian, Winston S. Churchill, use of the name in the
post-war years was not prolific, nor has it staged a
revival either in England or Scotland, the homeland of
his wife Clementine. It is a curious fact that coloured
families in Britain and America make more use of the
name. Winnie is a pet name.

Y

YOLANDE (f) Gr., meaning 'violet flower'. The Latin
form, *Violente*, influenced the French *Iolanthe*. There
was a St Jolantha in Spain in the thirteenth century
and the name was used by Hungarian royalty. Jolan or
Yolanda, a daughter of Andrew II of Hungary, married
James I, King of Arragon, who died in 1296. Yolanda
and Iolanda are currently in use in Scotland. Recorded
variants are Yalonda, Yulanda and Ylonda. The French
diminutive Yolette is occasionally found. Pet forms are
Yoe and Yola.

YVONNE (f) O.Fr. feminine form of Yvon or Ivon, probably derived from the Teutonic *Iv*, 'yew wood'. It is
sometimes considered to be the feminine form of the
Breton name Yves, uncommon in Britain, but Yvette is

in current use. The name Yvonne became fashionable at the beginning of the present century, and is well used in Scotland. Variants are Yvone, Evon and Evonne.

Z

ZACHARY (m) Heb., 'Jehovah has remembered'. In biblical times and later, the Latin form Zacharius was in use, but Zachary was occasionally used in the Middle Ages. Zacharius, a priest with a wife ELISABETH, both of them well beyond the normal child-producing years, through divine intervention had a son JOHN, who became John the Baptist (NT, Luke 1:5–17). There was, moreover, Zechariah, a prophet of the late sixth century, whose *Old Testament* book relates visions of a new world order and a nameless Messiah. The name was in vogue after the Reformation, but has declined in the present century. Zachary Boyd (1585–1653), a Scottish divine and author, was minister of Barony parish, Glasgow, and three times rector of the University of Glasgow. A late use of Zacharius is shown in the Maxwell family of Pollock. Zacharius Maxwell of Blawarthill was father of Sir John Maxwell of Pollock (1686–1752), an advocate at the Scottish bar. In America, the actor Zachary Scott (1914–65) probably influenced use of the name. In Scott's *Bride of Lammermoor*, Father Zachary was

the hermit to whom Raymond of Ravenswood con-
fessed his association with the mermaid of the well.
The Gaelic form of the name is Sachairi.

ZARA (f) Arabic, meaning 'splendour of the east'. It has
been suggested that the name is a variant of SARA. In
European literature it usually refers to an Arabian prin-
cess. William Congreve (1670–1729) used the name
for an African queen in his *Mourning Bride* (1697).
It was almost unknown in Scotland before Princess
Anne (now the Princess Royal) and her first husband,
Capt. Mark Phillips, named a daughter Zara in 1981.
Twenty-one girls received the name in 1990.

ZOE (f) Gr., meaning 'life'. The Jews of Alexandria used
the name to translate the Hebrew Eve into Greek: Eve
being esteemed as the mother of life. St Zoe was a
third-century martyr. The name came late to Britain,
probably in the mid-nineteenth century. Curiously it is
uncommon in literature, but it does appear in *Arethusa*,
a novel by Francis Marion Crawford (1854–1909). The
dieresis above the final vowel in his Zoë, has prompted
some parents to prefer the spellings Zoey, Zoie, Zowie
and Zoee, but Zoe is still the most popular choice.

Scottish Family History Societies

Aberdeen and N.E. Scotland FHS
FH Research Centre and Shop
164 King Street, Aberdeen AB2 3BD

Alloway and Ayrshire FHS
c/o Alloway Public Library,
Doonhom Road, Alloway KA7 4QQ

Arran FHS
c/o Rita Salman, Bracklin Grove
Corrie, Isle of Arran

Borders FHS
Miss Catherine Fish, the Toll House
Maxton, Melrose
Roxburgh TD6 0RL

Central Scotland FHS
Secretary, 19 Craigninnan Gardens
Dollar FK14 7JA

Dumfries & Galloway FHS
Secretary, Kylea, Corsock, Castle Douglas
Kirkcudbrightshire DG7 3DN

East Ayrshire FHS
c/o Dick Library, Elmbank Avenue
Kilmarnock KA1 3BU

Fife FHS
Mrs Janet Ross, 30 Duddingston Drive
Kirkcaldy KY2 6JP

Glasgow and West of Scotland FHS
Unit 5, 22 Mansfield Street
Glasgow G11 5QP

Hamilton & District FHS
c/o Central Library, 98 Cadzow Street
Hamilton ML3 6HQ

Highland FHS
Secretary, c/o Public Library,
Farraline Park, Inverness IV1 1NH

Largs and N. Ayrshire FHS
Secretary, 2 Raillies Road
Largs KA30 8QZ

The Lothians FHS
c/o Lasswade High School Centre, Eskdale Drive
Bonnyrigg EH19 24A

Orkney FHS
contact Mrs M.A. Scott, Lecknelm,
Annfield Crescent, Kirkwall, Orkney KW15 1NS

Perth and Kinross FHS
c/o AK Bell Library, York Place
Perth PH2 8EP

Scottish Genealogy Society
Library & FH Centre
15 Victoria Terrace, Edinburgh EH1 2JL

Shetland FHS
6 Hillhead, Lerwick
Shetland ZE1

Tay Valley FHS
FH Research Centre, 179 Princes Street
Dundee DD4 6DQ

Troon & District FHS
Contact: c/o MERC, Troon Public Library
South Beach, Troon, Ayrshire KA10 6EF

Scottish Association of FHS
Contact: 51/3 Mortonhall Road
Edinburgh EH9 2HN

Readers who wish ancestry research undertaken
on a professional basis should write to:

The Association of Scottish Genealogists and
Records Agents
Contact: Alan J. L. MacLeod (Chairman)
51/3 Mortonhall Road
Edinburgh EH9 2HN

All members adhere to a strict Code of Practice.

Principal Sources

ANDERSON, William, *The Scottish Nation*. 3 vols. Edinburgh & London: A. Fullarton & Co., 1878–80.

BLACK, George F., *The Surnames of Scotland: Their Origin, Meaning and History*. New York: N.Y. Public Library, 1946. Reprinted by Birlinn.

DALRYMPLE, Sir David, *Annals of Scotland, 1057–1371*. 3rd edition, 3 vols. Edinburgh: Constable 1819.

DICKINSON, William Croft (ed.), *The Sheriff Court Book of Fife, 1515–22*. Edinburgh: Scottish History Society, 1928.

DOUGLAS, Sir Robert, *The Baronage of Scotland*. 2nd edition, Edinburgh & London: Bell & Bradfute, and others 1798.

DOWDEN, John, *The Bishops of Scotland*, edited by J. Maitland Thomson. Glasgow: James Maclehose & Sons 1912.

EYRE & SPOTTISWOODE (Printers). *The Holy Bible, containing the Old and New Testaments* [King James version]. London 1877.

GILES, J.A. (Ed.), *Venerable Bede's Ecclesiastical History of England*, and *The Anglo-Saxon Chronicle*. London: Henry G. Bohn, 1847.

JOYCE, P.W., *The Origin and History of Irish Names and Places*. Dublin: McGlashan & Gill, 1875.

LAING David, (Collector), *The Laing Charters, 854–1837*, edited by Rev. John Anderson. Edinburgh: James Thin, 1899.

LAURIE, Sir Archibald C., *Early Scottish Charters*, prior to AD 1153. Glasgow: James Maclehose & Sons, 1905.

LOCKHART, J.G., *Memoirs of the Life of Sir Walter Scott, Baronet*. New edition in one volume. Edinburgh: Robert Cadell, 1845.

LOGAN, James, and McIan, R.R., *The Clans of the Scottish Highlands*. London: Ackerman & Co., 1845.

McBAIN, Alexander, 'The Old Gaelic System of Personal Names', in *Transactions of the Gaelic Society of Inverness, vol. xx (1894–6)*.

PAUL, Sir James Balfour (Ed.), *The Scots Peerage*. 9 vols. Edinburgh: David Douglas, 1904–14.

REEVES, Dr William (Ed.), *Life of St Columba*, by Adamnan. Edinburgh (Historians of Scotland series): Edmonston & Douglas, 1874.

REGISTRAR GENERAL FOR SCOTLAND, Office of *Personal Names in Scotland*. Edinburgh: General Register Office, 1991.

Ross, Andrew, and Grant, Francis J. (Eds.), *Alexander Nisbet's Heraldic Plates, originally intended for his 'System of Heraldy'*. Edinburgh: George Waterson & Sons, 1892.

Skene, William F, *Celtic Scotland: A History of Ancient Alban*. 3 vols. Edinburgh: David Douglas, 1886–90.

Taylor, A.B., 'Old Norse Nicknames in Scotland', in *The Scottish Genealogist*, Vol. 1, Nos. 1–3 (1954).

Watson, William J., *The History of the Celtic Place-Names of Scotland*. Edinburgh: William Blackwood & Sons, 1926. Reprinted by Birlinn.

Whitaker, Ian R., 'Colloquial Naming', in *The Scottish Genealogist*, vol. 2–3 (1954).